MAKING SENSE
OF SUFFERING

MAKING SENSE
OF SUFFERING

WAYNE E. BRICKEY

**DESERET
BOOK**

SALT LAKE CITY, UTAH

Library of Congress Cataloging-in-Publication Data

Brickey, Wayne E.
    Making sense of suffering / Wayne E. Brickey.
      p.   cm.
    Includes bibliographical references and index.
    ISBN 1-57008-721-0
    1. Suffering—Religious aspects—Church of Jesus Christ of Latter-day Saints.   2. Church of Jesus Christ of Latter-day Saints—Doctrines.   I. Title.
    BX8643.S93 B75 2001
    248.8'6—dc21

                2001002776

Printed in the United States of America   72082-6874
Publishers Press, Salt Lake City, Utah

10 9 8 7 6 5 4 3 2 1

To my mother
Marjorie

and to my wife
Joanne

Contents

Preface xi

Acknowledgments xiii

Introduction 1

THE GIFT OF GROWTH

 1 Keeping Estates 7

 2 Partway Will Never Do 9

 3 Here We Lay the Foundation 13

 4 The Firmness of Law 16

 5 Visiting Here in Weakness 19

 6 Suffering in the Shadows of Evil 22

 7 The Trial of the Innocent 24

 8 The Last Days of the World 27

 9 Our Dramatic Descent 29

10 Glimpses of Growth 31

"ENDURE IT WELL"

11 Momentary but Momentous 39

12 He Searches the Heart 42

13 Do This with Thy Might 45

14 Faith Fullness 48

15 Calm at the Core 51

16 Be of Good Cheer 54

17 The Second Yes 57

18 "In the Day of Adversity Consider" 60

19 Dispelling Fear Ahead of Time 63

20 Glimpses of Integrity 66

BENEATH WATCHFUL EYES

21 The Worth and Joy of Souls 77

22 The Pains of All Men 80

23 He Chastens 83

24 He Delivers 86

25 Guiding Us to Plan A 89

26 Surrounded by Angels 92

27 His Comfort 95

28 The Privilege and Price of Friendship 98

29 Suggestions for the Friends of Job 101

30 Glimpses of Grace 106

"GOD SHALL EXALT THEE"

31 Avoid the Greater Suffering 119

32 Stronger and Stronger 122

33 The Inward Miracle 125

34 Precious Is the Death of His Saints 128

35 He Offers His All 131

36 He Will Wipe Away the Tears 134

37 Linked to Him 137

38 The Faithful Crossing 140

39 A Perfect Schoolhouse 143

40 Glimpses of Glory 147

Sources 153

Index 155

Preface

J esus had arrived by boat along the northwestern shore of the Sea of
Galilee, met by an expectant multitude. One man in particular sought the
Lord in a state of emergency. Jairus, a local religious leader full of faith,
begged Jesus to come immediately to his home, where his twelve-year-old
daughter lay that very moment on the brink of death.

Jesus was willing, but progress to the home seemed slow. "Why," Jairus
may have wondered, "could Jesus not attend to other needs after meeting my
little girl's crisis, in which every minute is critical?"

Then came the crushing message while Jesus and Jairus were yet en
route: "Thy daughter is dead." The Master was unruffled by the news, but
what of Jairus? Would he bolt for home in agony or would he, despite his
grief, continue to trust the slow and confident pace at which the Master was
moving? "Be not afraid," Jesus reassured him, "only believe."

The scene on the cover of this book breaks into the drama in the home of
Jairus at that long and lonely moment before divine help is poured out. Jairus,
not with his daughter for her last breath, has belatedly joined his heartbroken
wife. The tumult of the doubters still echoes in their stricken minds as their

child's pathetic little body lies cold, limp, and pallid before them. Soon they will sing with untold rejoicing, but for now they are wracked with grief, hardly comprehending that in a moment her life will be restored. The Lord stands near the scene, watching carefully, poised to bless when he sees fit (Mark 5:22–24, 35–42; Luke 8:40–42, 49–56).

The suspended and aching moment faced by Jairus and his wife resembles moments we all face. We sorrow over what is, but we anticipate with faith what soon will be.

WAYNE E. BRICKEY

The center of the painting features the daughter's lifeless hand in the clinging grip of her mother. The daughter's deathbed is reminiscent of an altar; her parents must decide whether they will submit to a higher will. What has been taken from them and what is eventually taken from us—our life or the life of a loved one—we relinquish, willingly or unwillingly. I believe that Jairus, his wife, and even the little twelve-year-old maid were willing to submit to the will of the Lord, whatever it might have been.

The doorway through which the Lord enters the scene, the place from which greater light floods in, is the ever-present veil he parts when he perceives that we are ready.

JOSEPH BRICKEY

Acknowledgments

This book owes its existence to my wife, Joanne, who has long felt that I should write it. She has gently passed this conviction along to our children, who have encouraged me without the slightest question. One of our children, Joseph, has lent his steady and gifted hand to this book with inspiring art.

I thank Cory Maxwell, manager of the Deseret Book imprint, for his always-refreshing honesty, gentle wisdom mingled with keen professionalism, and insistence that a book have a mission. I also appreciate the sincere manner in which his coworkers have prepared this book for its errand.

This book is laced together by statements from the prophets, to whom I owe a great debt. Were the windows of higher truth closed, I would see sense in very few things, least of all suffering.

Light from those windows has become visible only by falling upon real lives—the sufferers I have watched up close and from afar. I thank them for their decisions, hour-by-hour, to react with faith to their pain. Among those sufferers is one in particular who will, in time, make sense of everything. I acknowledge him most of all.

Introduction

Is mortal suffering really part of the plan of happiness?[1] Are misery and woe really necessary during our earthly probation?[2] It would seem so, for we are all surrounded by affliction. Fortunately, our affliction is but a small moment, sandwiched between two eternities.

Where is the God of love when suffering occurs? That question resounds in the moans of human history. Even an agonized Joseph Smith pleaded in prayer, "O God, where art thou?"[3]

The God of perfect love is a God of perfect wisdom, and he is nearby. But his plan permits suffering in his universe. Without apology, he keeps sending his spirit children into the thick of things. In his long view, suffering makes sense. It can never make much sense to us, however, until we see things his way.

Oddly enough, our vision sometimes improves when our conditions worsen, creating an occasional windowpane, or window of pain, in the veil. A paralyzing problem can bring the stillness that causes us to pause and, for a change, reverently look at the whole scene, which is the smallest scene we can trust.

Of course, mere thoughts about suffering, such as the ones in this book, cannot replace suffering itself. On the other hand, suffering itself is no replacement for thought. A clarifying lesson every now and then can do wonders for a dreary laboratory. In the end, we need both pain and pondering.

> *It is important that we should understand the reasons and causes of our exposure to the vicissitudes of life and of death, and the designs and purposes of God in our coming into the world, our sufferings here, and our departure hence. . . . It is a subject we ought to study. . . . If we have any claim on our Heavenly Father for anything, it is for knowledge on this important subject.*[4]

This dispensation pours out a flood of light by which we can make some sense of suffering. Sacred literature, echoed by private experience, gives comfort and perspective. Making sense of suffering means gaining reassurance until God wipes away all tears. Meanwhile, we may wipe away despair.

God grants mortal suffering because it can do wonders for us. It is a brief gift from his gentle hand. When the gift has passed, our concerns will be resolved. Until then, our work is to resolve our hearts toward the will of God and his Son. They are watching more closely and with greater concern than we realize.

Mortal suffering makes lasting improvements in the eternal self. It turns up the volume on God's voice to us, and it turns up the volume on our pleadings to him.

This little book is offered in the belief that suffering deserves thought. After all, life on earth is our one chance in the middle of eternity to learn from this brief gift. We might as well receive it as given: thoughtfully.

Notes

1. Alma 42:8, 16.
2. Moses 6:48.
3. D&C 121:1.
4. Joseph Smith, *Teachings of the Prophet Joseph Smith,* 324.

The Gift of Growth

We will forever need the lessons and patience gained in mortality. Earthborn wisdom must never dim in any mind. Mortal growth, which comes from curing or enduring problems, is for the eons. What would be the use of an easy and forgettable mortal life? Between eternity past and eternity future, we come here to receive the gift of growth. It awaits us all.

1

Keeping Estates

On a clear night, when we look up at the ancient lights burning deep in space, we see something of ourselves. We too are ancient. He who fires each of those magnificent stars made you and me to become beings of glory.

Only by God's devoted support may we pass through the long process of becoming like him. He provides all the conditions we need for growth in our second estate. As suggested by words like *stable, state, stay,* and *steady,* an estate is a place of fixed conditions.[1] The conditions of progress that God, at his infinite expense, grants to us in this life include working laws, building materials, saving powers, and second chances. To all of this we must add our consent and hard work.

To keep an estate, we must become as dependable as the laws themselves—keeping trusts and holding a steady course no matter what. Integrity, or being true, is the way we keep an estate and enjoy all its blessings.

And they who keep their first estate shall be added upon; . . . and they who keep their second estate shall have glory added upon their heads for ever and ever.[2]

The laws of the first estate were bathed in light. Free of darkness, sorrow, and pain, we kept those laws and grew in glory. The greater blessings of the second estate, however, are offered under different conditions.

An enemy roams here in our second estate, "going to and fro in the earth."[3] He who failed so bitterly in his first estate now urges us, amid our mortal sufferings, to do what he would do—doubt, dispute, despair, disobey, and darken.[4]

On the other hand, we can turn to one who "is able to keep [us] from falling, and to present [us] faultless before the presence of his glory with exceeding joy."[5] He does not apologize for the harsh conditions of our second estate. He is the great keeper of all estates. He pleads with us to keep our blessings by keeping his way, his paths, and our covenants with him.[6]

Behold, I am with thee, and will keep thee in all places whither thou goest, . . . for I will not leave thee, until I have done that which I have spoken to thee of.[7]

Let him keep you.

Notes

1. *Noah Webster's First Edition,* s.v. "Stable," "State," "Stay," "Steady."
2. Abraham 3:26.
3. Job 1:7.
4. Moses 4:4.
5. Jude 1:24.
6. D&C 35:24; Helaman 5:12.
7. Genesis 28:15.

2

Partway Will Never Do

Happiness is the object and design of our existence; and will be the end thereof, if we pursue the path that leads to it; and this path is virtue, uprightness, faithfulness, holiness, and keeping all the commandments of God.[1]

J oseph Smith's oft-quoted statement defining the path leading to happiness does not list comfort and pleasure. They may not block our way, of course, but they could. At any rate, Joseph does not mention them as necessary. Nor does any other prophet. And that is just as well because many mortals have been deprived of pleasure and even comfort. We must believe that the many lives now filled with pain are headed for happiness later on, and that many lives filled with pleasure are headed elsewhere.

In Eden a particular fruit brought toil and trouble. Before eating that fruit, Adam and Eve, in the divine image, were safe. But they could not become exalted like God unless they partook. It was as if a steep path led from the safe to the celestial, from the garden to the mountain, from Eden to Zion.

Trials and adversity can be preparatory to becoming born anew.[2]

Suffering places us behind a door and hides us somewhat from the view of others. The privacy allows adjustment, renewal, and transformation. The fortunate interruption allows us to break old chains. When we emerge, we need not put them back on. In this way we discover meaning in suffering, and that life's troubles are worth the trouble. Friends and loved ones will be quietly relieved that the pain recreated us. But we need more than a brief pause behind the door of suffering.

Poisons stored in the soul, foreign and forgotten, must be forced into circulation. We must sweat them out, and such perspiration takes time. The change must be whole. Whatever else suffering may be, it is never a waste of time. In the months it took to walk the plains and mountains, the pioneers were free to revise their souls—the very reason we enter mortality.

Every trial and experience you have passed through is necessary for your salvation.[3]

Like millions who have trodden the winepress before, we face the unfamiliar with faith. Abraham walked by faith through foreign places. He went from a stifling past to a holy future. Of course, he did not *have* to exercise faith or benefit from the path. His father, Terah, came along for the trip and had the same chance to change but refused.[4]

My people must be tried in all things, that they may be prepared to receive the glory that I have for them, even the glory of Zion.[5]

The costs of the journey are handled chiefly by Christ. So we try to comprehend his sacrifice, deserve his mercy, and always remember him. But what remains? What is our part of the cost? In fees of faith and fortitude, we simply give all we have, which heals and purifies. He who asks for our little "all" will greet us after our return to him and will give us his infinite "all."[6]

I have decreed in my heart, saith the Lord, that I will prove you in all things, whether you will abide in my covenant, even unto death, that you may be found worthy.[7]

Billions press forward from the premortal world, yearning to pay the full fare. Once they arrive, their yearning is visible: the husband yearning to provide, the wife yearning to give birth, the child yearning to grow, the student yearning to study. The offspring of God crave to give their all, to pay full fare. And well they should. In exchange, they gain their souls.

What shall a man give in exchange for his soul?[8]

The splendid place we seek is high up. When the steep path to God presents itself, we should wisely give our all. Part fare will never do, for partway to his presence is not far enough.

Notes

1. Joseph Smith, *Teachings of the Prophet Joseph Smith*, 255–56.
2. James E. Faust, "The Refiner's Fire," *Ensign,* May 1979, 54.
3. Brigham Young, *Journal of Discourses,* 8:150.
4. Abraham 1:16; 2:1–5.
5. D&C 136:31.
6. D&C 76:95; 84:38.
7. D&C 98:14.
8. Matthew 16:26.

3

Here We Lay the Foundation

We will have to go even beyond the grave before we reach that perfection and shall be like God. But here we lay the foundation.[1]

Trouble is an essential part of the plan of salvation for the same reason that buildings require a foundation. The base we build in this life stays with us ever after. Preparing to meet God is deep work. Perhaps finishing touches can be added later, but the foundation, including patience and cheer, must be set early.

All the people shouted with a great shout . . . because the foundation of the house of the Lord was laid.[2]

Because it finishes the beginning and undergirds the future, a solid foundation is something to shout about. Nephi could make a holy book because affliction prepared him to know God.[3] Solomon said the price of much wisdom is much grief.[4]

Alma . . . beheld that their afflictions had truly humbled them, and that they were in a preparation to hear the word.[5]

The word can transform us but only when we are ready. Tribulation often precedes the voice of God, in Church history and in private life. The foundation is not laid in easy steps. In any case, mortal life makes these steps possible.

Your body really is the instrument of your mind and the foundation of your character.[6]

To build, eternal beings enter mortal bodies. The embodied spirit, like it or not, is apprised of all sorts of bodily conditions. Busy nerve endings are nearly everywhere, speaking the loud language of distress. Other afflictions, not so physical, also pierce the spirit-self. One example is loneliness. Others are embarrassment, bondage, grief, or guilt. These can be more bitter than physical pain. For many people, pain of some kind throbs around-the-clock.

Because we are "fearfully and wonderfully made,"[7] mortal life is both overwhelming and undergirding. But when the healing comes, our bodies will be abodes of joy and glory. For now, mortal experience is preparing us.[8]

Notes

1. Joseph Fielding Smith, *Doctrines of Salvation,* 2:18.
2. Ezra 3:11.
3. 1 Nephi 1:1.
4. Ecclesiastes 1:18.

5. Alma 32:6.

6. Boyd K. Packer, "Ye Are the Temple of God," *Ensign,* November 2000, 72.

7. Psalm 139:14.

8. Alma 34:32.

4

The Firmness of Law

If all the righteous were protected and the wicked destroyed, the whole program of the Father would be annulled.[1]

The universe seems unfriendly at times. Real life is dangerous, for law itself is firm and unyielding. But the laws that make an engine stop without fuel are the very laws that make it run *with* fuel. The laws that enable a cancer cell to grow empower *any* cell to grow. So, the unbending universe *is* friendly . . . to law.

And some laws are more important than others. God whispers these within us. We may shout down the inner voice for a time, but he never approves evil. Long after mischief has run its wild course, conscience will live on, still breathing his quiet truth.

Sometimes we try to sneak around law. Suffering teaches us to stop sneaking around and to hearken to the whispering God of truth. Suffering teaches us that law is the fixed path to results. We get the results only if we do what causes the results. Fixed law may confine, even punish. But only fixed law permits life and joy.

Law also guarantees variety. Do *this* and get one result. Do *that* and get quite another. Lehi calls this *opposition*.[2] Opposite causes yield opposite results. Eat bread and get one result; eat a rock and get another. Turn left and go to point A; turn right and go to point B.

Suppose that suddenly there were no opposition. You would get the same result regardless of your choices. This sameness in all things would be a prison. If all causes brought the same result, effect would be canceled, as would change and action, energy and substance. Instead of living in a universe of choices and results, you could choose nothing but point A.

Lehi described this situation perfectly as "a compound in one."[3] Satan once offered to imprison us in such a compound. He offered to remove risk, but he really meant to remove freedom. His system seemed safe only because it was no system at all. It was a fraud.[4]

On the other hand, the Father desires us to be free, no matter what the price. His plan is full of big possibilities, including dangerous possibilities. He knew that free beings would break some laws before mastering them. The penalties would be costly, especially for the Son, who would answer the law as a proxy for lawbreakers.

> *Behold, he offereth himself a sacrifice for sin, to answer the ends of the law, unto all those who have a broken heart and a contrite spirit.*[5]

The firm universe is softened because of the Atonement. What would have extinguished us educates us instead. We are free to explore laws and conquer our flaws.

Because that they are redeemed from the fall they have become free forever.[6]

Christ absorbs the brunt of our mistakes, leaving just enough tragedy for our growth and learning. He also permits delay. Lawful results come gradually rather than with lightning speed. The righteous may be blessed long after obedience. During the delay, they may suffer. By contrast, the wicked often experience misleading satisfaction for a season. But law catches up—firmly and finally. It just gives us time to decide to do right for the right reasons.

Notes

1. Spencer W. Kimball, *Teachings of Spencer W. Kimball,* 77.
2. 2 Nephi 2:11.
3. 2 Nephi 2:11.
4. 2 Nephi 2:12; 9:8–10; Moses 4:3.
5. 2 Nephi 2:7.

5

Visiting Here in Weakness

A rare golfer may finish a round with fewer strokes than expected. But no one gets through eighteen holes with seventeen strokes. The mortal course is just plain rough, and we come to it frail and ill equipped. Trouble is "par for the course," as the golfer might say.

> *Many of the righteous shall fall a prey to disease, to pestilence, etc., by reason of the weakness of the flesh, and yet be saved in the Kingdom of God.*[1]

God is able to make a perfect world, or he could not make a world at all. A billion wonders per moment blend into a working system of precise timing, light, and life—proof that the Creator can do anything. He can make any lawful system his judgment prescribes.

So why all the disease and deformity? Why, with all that adequate power, does God not move things to the next level? Why does he permit dreadful unfairness and accident? Clearly, he expects the mortal phase to be thorny, imperfect, and encumbered with injustice. He has made things precisely as they should be for now—perfectly imperfect! Of course, those few things that should never fail, never do. And what ought to go awry does so in just the right way.

> *Because that Adam fell, we are; and by his fall came death; and we are made partakers of misery and woe.*[2]

From the Fall, we inherit fragile bodies, touchy nerves, foggy minds, and fearful hearts. Suffering is in our blood. We take on the firmness of law while at our worst. It is nice to know that was the plan all along. If life is hard, the plan is working.

That same plan arranged for a heavenly covering—the Atonement—to comfort us in the flood of woe. "Atonement" comes from the Hebrew *kippur* or *kaphar*—to cover or protect.[3] It is our mantle in a cold world, a wondrous layer that makes all the difference.

That covering helped Adam and Eve survive the invasive sorrows of the Fall and the prying sabotage of Satan. Genesis says the Lord "clothed" them with coats of skins.[4] In supposing that animals were sacrificed to provide this covering, we are reminded of the real covering: the Atonement provided by the Lamb of God.

God could easily disarm the thorny nature around us, but he is not going to do so in this life. Though we face the lawful universe in temporal weakness, the temporal is only temporary. Things will not stay this way. Beginning with death, they start to improve dramatically. Death, the most mortal part of mortality, concludes and fulfills our visit here in weakness.[5]

Notes

1. Joseph Smith, *Teachings of the Prophet Joseph Smith*, 162.
2. Moses 6:48.
3. James Strong, *A Concise Dictionary*, s.v. "3722"; H. W. F. Gesenius, *Gesenius' Hebrew and Chaldee Lexicon*, s.v. "3725."
4. Genesis 3:21.
5. 2 Nephi 9:6–7.

6
Suffering in the Shadows of Evil

Even without evil, suffering would abound in the fallen world. But evil makes things profoundly worse. The destroyer stands grinning in nearby shadows, scheming evil, plotting out miserable outcomes. He spies, intrudes, rages at our heels, and strikes when we are weak. Letting us live our own lives is out of the question. He delights in torment. He has no remorse.[1] Until he is out of the way, we must stand firm.

And he beheld Satan; and he had a great chain in his hand, and it veiled the whole face of the earth with darkness; and he looked up and laughed, and his angels rejoiced.[2]

To Satan, our destruction is a personal matter. The Hebrew root of his name means opponent or archenemy.[3] Satan hates God and the faithful. Spite is his specialty and his addiction. If we are drawn into contention, we become bound, link by link, by his heavy chains. On the other hand, we can keep ourselves free of dark ideas and intentions by drawing nigh unto the one who is far greater than our personal enemy.

And it shall come to pass in that day that his burden shall be taken away from off thy shoulder, and his yoke from off thy neck, and the yoke shall be destroyed because of the anointing.[4]

Of course, people can spread sorrow without the slightest help from Satan. Vain and possessive leaders can set in motion forces that are beyond their understanding or control.[5] When humans turn away from light, their culture—be it in the home or the nation—darkens and degrades. Much suffering can be traced to these shadows. God lets the abused suffer for a time and then restores and compensates them tenderly. He does not let the abuser off so easily.

The God of peace shall bruise Satan under your feet shortly.[6]

If we are good, we will only experience the pain we need during our visit to the shadows. When we leave, we will find ourselves in a new relationship with the evil one. Our old oppressor will not simply be at bay but will lie conquered beneath our feet.[7]

Notes

1. D&C 10:26–27; Moses 6:15.
2. Moses 7:26.
3. James Strong, *A Concise Dictionary*, s.v. "7854"; H. W. F. Gesenius, *Gesenius' Hebrew and Chaldee Lexicon*, s.v. "7854."
4. 2 Nephi 20:27.
5. Alma 46:9.
6. Romans 16:20.
7. Revelation 12:10–11.

7

The Trial of the Innocent

On one occasion during the time of Jesus, Roman soldiers slew a number of Jewish worshippers on the temple grounds.[1] Knowing that his audience was prone to draw the wrong conclusion from such tragedies, Jesus asked, "Suppose ye that these Galileans were sinners above all the Galileans, because they suffered such things?" Should we look upon tragedy as punishment? Does one person suffer more than others because he is not as good? The Master settled the question simply: "I tell you, Nay."[2]

Consider Job. In his day, no better man lived on earth. Yet no one suffered more. He learned that there is such a thing as "the trial of the innocent."[3]

Trials are explorations of strength. But because they stretch us, trials do not just check for strength, they add strength. Trials also deepen our search for depth. Trials do this for the innocent as well as for the guilty.

Our mortal suffering began with all the discomfort and trauma of our birth at a time when we were pure as heaven. We were not being punished. Rather, we were, even then, already being pushed. Our quest requires pain. It is a weapon in the battle against our lesser traits.

One way the innocent are tried is by the acts of imperfect people around them. Friendships falter and careless words seem unfair. But the Master invites us at such times to react in gentle, nonblaming ways.

> *Blessed are ye when men shall revile you, and persecute you, and shall say all manner of evil against you falsely, for my sake. . . . Rejoice, and be exceeding glad.*[4]

When others help us heal, they too may suffer in some way. Suffering is the modest price of real friendship. Parents, leaders, and teachers who quietly pay this price day and night for their children and their charges are true friends.

Through the innocent suffering of Jesus, we become innocent ourselves. So if we must suffer, let it be innocently.

> *It is better . . . that ye suffer for well doing, than for evil doing.*[5]

Mortal eye cannot foresee, and mortal mind cannot imagine the far-reaching results of our innocent suffering. It touches too many lives. It reaches too far into future worlds. It is not a badge of shame. It will, at last, sanctify and dignify us.[6]

Notes

1. Luke 13:1; Bruce R. McConkie, *The Mortal Messiah*, 3:193–94.
2. Luke 13:2–3.
3. Job 9:23.

4. Matthew 5:11–12.
5. 1 Peter 3:17.
6. Romans 8:17–18; 1 Peter 4:12–19; D&C 133:45.

8

The Last Days of the World

Darkness covereth the earth, and gross darkness the minds of the people. . . . A day of wrath, . . . of weeping, of mourning, and of lamentation; and as a whirlwind [vengeance] shall come.[1]

Innocent suffering cannot be relieved as long as the vast, victimizing culture known as Babylon, or the world, persists. This sinister system will not calmly go away. God himself must vanquish it. A divine broom will prepare for the reign of peace. Until then, the empire of selfishness, conflict, and sorrow will live out its last days. Hearts will continue to harden and break. Satan's twisted dreams will seem to come true.[2]

The Lord will lay mighty hands upon the nations, not only to humble and awaken but also to heal. His judgments will soften hearts and stir repentance so that his blood may cleanse.

Latter-day sorrow will spread beyond the wicked. But severe trouble here and there among the faithful will knit them together as one. Their master bids them not to be afraid. In their gatherings they will find refuge from the storm and keep their appointment with his peace.[3]

It is my testimony that we are facing difficult times. . . . We will be called upon to prove our spiritual stamina, for the days ahead will be filled with affliction and difficulty.[4]

Our dramatic opportunity to minister to mankind is the silver lining in the brooding storm clouds. Our tears and prayers and labors for others will make a difference. We will "comfort those that stand in need of comfort, and . . . stand as witnesses of God" in doing so.[5] If they receive comfort, they may also receive testimony, and their worst moments may pave the way for their best moments.

O Lord, we delight not in the destruction of our fellow men; their souls are precious before thee.[6]

Thus, Christ and his elect people will soften and shorten the last days of an unhappy world. Then suffering will cease.[7]

Notes

1. D&C 112:23–24.
2. D&C 1:35–36; 88:89–93.
3. 1 Nephi 22:14–19.
4. James E. Faust, "That We Might Know Thee," *Ensign*, January 1999, 5.
5. Mosiah 18:9.
6. D&C 109:43.
7. Joseph Smith–Matthew 1:20.

9

Our Dramatic Descent

Myriad beings live in the broad universe. Only a few are mortal at any one time. This low, second estate is a strange and solemn condition. To those who watch from above, we are a remarkable sight.

The Lord possessed me in the beginning of his way, before his works of old. . . .
While as yet he had not made the earth. . . . When he prepared the heavens, I
was there. . . . Then I was by him, as one brought up with him: and I was daily
his delight, rejoicing always before him.[1]

In the home we came from, we were royal and lovable, our Father's delight. But we were not complete. We needed to be stretched. So we set crowns aside and descended, forgetting all.[2]

Yet there are reminders. For example, the sick person who does not feel royal is treated as a king or queen when anointed—a good time to be reminded!

To beings of other worlds, our ills are high drama. We are like bewildered patients, but they see why surgery is needed. Many of them were once in our place, and memory makes them gentle nurses indeed.

My Spirit shall be in your hearts, and mine angels round about you, to bear you up.[3]

We cannot see what other eternal beings see, but we can at least believe what they see. A gospel outlook sweetens our brief, dramatic descent.

Some of our present circumstances may reflect previous agreements, now forgotten, but once freely made.[4]

Shocking dramas unfold around our homes and sometimes in them. Had we understood then what we experience now, we might have frozen at the starting line instead of taking the first step forward. But we embarked, setting out on a voyage of riveting reversals and magnificent memories. Even as we ponder all this, the same God who pointed out the descending path to you and me is sending countless others to their own journeys full of surprises and growth.

Notes

1. Proverbs 8:22, 26–27, 30.
2. Abraham 3:24–25; Psalm 8:4–6; Matthew 18:10.
3. D&C 84:88.
4. Neal A. Maxwell, "The Great Plan of the Eternal God," *Ensign*, May 1984, 22.

10

Glimpses of Growth

The costs of growth are temporary; the results are eternal. No matter how much we know of this world's distress, we see only a tiny, stern episode in a long and marvelous story. We rarely get a hint of the completed product, the coming together of the premortal, mortal, and postmortal pieces of the puzzle. But now and then we get a peek at the wondrous growth going on.

Here are a few glimpses of growth from people of our time. Their stories represent but a sample of the countless untold stories of growth happening around us and, fortunately, within us.

The tears and horrors of child abuse darken much of the private history of mankind. One dark episode comes from Elena,[1] the child of a crime-ridden neighborhood in an unstable, uncaring nation. She was frequently violated in every way by adults and young ruffians alike. Suffocating feelings of worthlessness and horror blight her childhood memories. When she encountered the gospel, she believed its joyous claims. Instead of clinging to her bizarre past, Elena faced the light. Yet life still is not easy.

The gospel is wonderful, but it hasn't yet removed all the scars of my suffering. Sometimes the memories make it hard to be close to my Father in Heaven. But I'm getting better a tiny bit at a time, and I know it's because of him. I'm not giving up, and my Father in Heaven isn't giving up either.

Lehi's words to his young son Jacob, who had been mistreated by his elder brothers Laman and Lemuel, apply to all the abused. Rude afflictions will, by the slow and steady hand of God, be turned into "gain"—the growth for which earth life was designed.

In thy childhood thou hast suffered afflictions and much sorrow, because of the rudeness of thy brethren. Nevertheless, Jacob, my firstborn in the wilderness, thou knowest the greatness of God; and he shall consecrate thine afflictions for thy gain.[2]

From Marissa, whose adopted child was taken away:

I've found that suffering is easy to speak of theoretically. When heart-wrenching trials are thrown into an already semithorny path, the time for theorizing is over and the hard work begins.

In 1989 we had the privilege of adopting a beautiful baby boy. The joy that my husband and I and our four daughters experienced was inexpressible. Our love for him was immediate and deep. But then came the day when racial issues called into question the adoption proceedings. Our hearts froze; our lives froze. The unspeakable, horrifying outcome was that our son was taken from our

arms and our home, though we have never stopped holding him in our hearts
since that day. Our joy turned into anguish. We were left with broken hearts.
In total confusion, we asked, "Why?"

There were many days of suffering and pain yet ahead. But twelve years
later, my heart is filled with peace. We know the peace and spiritual growth
that seem to come only by suffering. How can we know how to succor others if
we have not experienced our own Gethsemane? How can we expect to receive
salvation if we have not experienced a small particle of what the Savior felt?

It is really possible to view this trial with peace and joy, for that is our view
of it today. I testify that faith and submissiveness are rocks that build a
fortress, assembled with love, long-suffering, trust, charity, prayer, scripture
study, service, and following prophets. Sadness can turn to joy and pain to
peace if we will turn our hearts to the Master.

From Rob, a burn victim:

Fourteen years ago, I was in an army helicopter that crashed and went up
in flames in the Mojave Desert. After two months, various surgeries, and many
painkillers and hallucinations, I found myself in the rehabilitation unit of the
Brooke Army Medical Center in San Antonio, Texas. I was scarred and
scared—physically, emotionally, and spiritually. The future loomed like a
great mysterious black hole that heightened my fears tremendously. I was

terribly angry inside. I had been doing all that had been spiritually asked of me, and now this. Why?

The LDS chaplain and full-time missionaries took turns bringing the sacrament to my room on Sundays. I had progressed sufficiently so that on one unforgettable Sunday they invited me to offer one of the sacrament prayers. We closed our eyes and I began, "Oh God . . ." Tears flowed and I couldn't say any more. The others in the room thought I was spiritually touched. But in reality I was so angry because of the "wrongs" my loving Heavenly Father had allowed to come into my and my young family's life. I could not at that moment humble myself sufficiently to address him reverently in the capacity of that sacrament prayer. With time, when my heart and attitudes had softened, I would come to enjoy many sweet comforts and spiritual healings, far surpassing any previous spiritual experiences.

These fourteen years have been long and rugged. But I would not now wish one thorn less on the path I've been on. The path has helped me to know that my Redeemer and my Heavenly Father live and love me. I have begun to really enjoy the peaceable things of the Spirit.

How is it done? How do we rise from the depths of anger and despair to the peace that surpasses understanding? We go to the source. We individually, with bended knee and contrite heart, plead with the Father in the name of our Savior to increase our faith, and to root out of our hearts anything that shouldn't be *there. I testify that the Lord does support those who love and serve him in their time of affliction and that he eases their burdens according to his infinite love and wisdom.*

From Karrie, who suffered severe pancreatitis immediately after giving birth to her second child:

I spent many months in the hospital, vacillating between life and death. My recovery was unbelievably slow, and it was very painful. I guess all this made it educational. Otherwise, I doubt if I would have grown much from it.

I was humbled because I wasn't in control. It seemed like everyone around me was managing my situation except for me. I felt like a child. And I had so little time with my little newborn, Emily. But I began to realize that there was still a whole eternity remaining for Emily and me.

I certainly discovered the goodness of others. There was the nurse who called my Relief Society compassionate service leader, even sent flowers, and in various ways went beyond her duties.

I don't miss the illness, but I miss the quality of thought. I was more removed from the world and its trivia. I felt more in tune with the Spirit. Things in the scriptures and conference talks hit me harder then. I saw more and had tender feelings when studying the gospel. When you're in such discomfort, you don't feel like thinking hard, but somehow your level of thought is on a higher plane. I might have more quantity of thought now that I'm well, but I miss the quality.

It seemed that others could tell I was close to the Spirit. More goodness radiated from me than usual. So it's hard to feel that my illness was a bad thing. I see things differently. I'm a better person, more soft around the edges than before. I find myself wanting to be a support to someone else.

It's almost a crutch to be sick like that! It can make you more tender and aware. I don't think most of us would turn out very well if we didn't get sick now and then.

Notes

1. Names have been changed.
2. 2 Nephi 2:1–2.

"ENDURE IT WELL"

The Lord urged his suffering servant Joseph Smith to "endure it well" (D&C 121:8). What does that mean? When the sobering gift of growth comes our way, how can we receive it with grace and integrity?

And there were gathered together in one place an innumerable company of the spirits of the just, who had been faithful in the testimony of Jesus while they lived in mortality; and who had offered sacrifice in the similitude of the great sacrifice of the Son of God, and had suffered tribulation in their Redeemer's name (D&C 138:12–13).

11

Momentary but Momentous

Mortality is like taking the business loop off a highway during a long journey. How you prepare during the stop will affect the next stage of your journey.

This life is the most vital period in our eternal existence.[1]

Mortality may also be compared to the brief time needed to purify gold or silver. What could not happen at normal temperatures takes place in a moment under extreme heat: the ore melts and impurities are released. We bring to the heat of mortality an ancient ore. Dramatic change unfolds as we take our turn in the fiery furnace of adversity under the eye of the Refiner.[2] Therefore, we need be mortal only once, and only briefly.

How long wilt thou hide thy face from me? How long shall I take counsel in my soul, having sorrow in my heart daily?[3]

Only eternity is a long time. All other periods are mere moments among the eons.[4]

A thousand years in thy sight are but as yesterday when it is past, and as a watch in the night.[5]

The painful moment may seem endless, but it is sure to pass. It must take its modest place alongside all other moments, stored with the tame and passive past. When we suffer, let us see the passing present as it is—destined to become a small part of the combined yesterdays.

If purified gold could speak, what would it say about the still and sluggish time it was held in the earth? "That is but as yesterday."

Our light affliction, which is but for a moment, worketh for us a far more exceeding and eternal weight of glory.[6]

Sorrow seems to move in slow motion. But when the moment has passed, we will move back into eternity with ease. Time will lose its hold on our minds, and we will behold the Eternal One.[7]

This life became a probationary state; a time to prepare to meet God.[8]

Notes

1. Joseph Fielding Smith, *Doctrines of Salvation,* 1:69.
2. Isaiah 48:10.
3. Psalm 13:1–2.
4. D&C 121:7–8.
5. Psalm 90:4.

6. 2 Corinthians 4:17.
7. D&C 88:49–50.
8. Alma 12:24.

12

He Searches the Heart

God seemed to spend a lot of time fussing and hovering over Job, training and trying him. Why was Job so interesting to the Lord?

What is man, that thou shouldest magnify him? And that thou shouldest set thine heart upon him? And that thou shouldest visit him every morning, and try him every moment?[1]

Job's suffering was part of some big project. He had vast potential not apparent to himself. The Lord was more devoted to Job's future than Job was. The only conflict between Job and his Creator was Job's reluctance to be made into something more than he already was. The Creator had great plans for Job, and he has great plans for us.

Each life's story is a serious one because our Creator has distinctly spiritual plans for us. The plot, unclear to us, makes perfect sense to him because he refuses to see our lives narrowly.

All things unto me are spiritual, and not at any time have I given unto you a law which was temporal. . . . For my commandments are spiritual.[2]

The spiritual is the permanent rather than the temporary. It is the entire, infinite picture, rather than the sliver we now see. The spiritual touches intangible processes and eternal outcomes that cause us to resemble God. The spiritual deals not just with spirit matter but also with all matters that are spiritual in their powers and possibilities. Mortal life touches this realm all day long.

I the Lord search the heart.[3]

God always sees this realm, mindful of how the temporal affects the permanent. He sees where things are headed. He scans the heart for spots that need cleaning, mending, building. Of course, these spots do not show up unless we are under some stress.

The Lord thy God led thee these forty years in the wilderness, to humble thee, and to prove thee, to know what was in thine heart.[4]

Even the most physical suffering is not strictly physical after all. It does not end in the physical realm where it began. It soaks into the heart and spreads. Suffering is finely connected to the versatile and permanent self, the spirit. Suffering is a spiritual matter.

God's view is so different from ours that his will often surprises us.

As the heavens are higher than the earth, so are my ways higher than your ways, and my thoughts than your thoughts.[5]

His galaxy-sized intentions are guaranteed to conflict with our little plans now and then.[6] If we will simply let his wisdom override ours, our uninspired goals will not restrict the story of our lives, and we will become his greatest miracles.

You will have all kinds of trials to pass through. And it is quite as necessary for you to be tried as it was for Abraham and other men of God and . . . God will feel after you.[7]

He feels after us. He searches our hearts with his.

Notes

1. Job 7:17–18.
2. D&C 29:34–35.
3. Jeremiah 17:10.
4. Deuteronomy 8:2.
5. Isaiah 55:9.
6. James 1:2–3.
7. Joseph Smith, cited by John Taylor, *Journal of Discourses*, 24:197.

13

Do This with Thy Might

The easy life, in excess, is a deadly, smothering prison. The hard life, on the other hand, quickens our heart rate and gives us the energy to live and breathe. Earth abounds in what we need most: work.

Let us labor diligently; . . . for we have a labor to perform whilst in this tabernacle of clay.[1]

Work is the proven key to life and growth. We see it all through God's nature and his kingdom. To be passive is to die, physically and spiritually. Thus, the Lord asks his people to leave the parlor and go to work.

Whatsoever thy hand findeth to do, do it with thy might.[2]

Hard work places before us something to tame—a horse, a stack of bills, a broken machine, or a room in disarray. But apart from the thing before us, we ourselves need to be tamed. If we have any lower tendencies—discouragement, guile, unkindness—they must go. Whatever the outward task, the inner taming is our real work. Enduring well makes us whole by awakening and taming our souls.

Taming is slow work, but the good news is that slow processes cannot be quickly undone. The greatest beings in eternity gained their high ground by going uphill one step at a time. Even our exemplar, Christ, grew in stages.[3]

Gethsemane is holy because of the whole offering made there. By the same principle, millions of other places, such as unheralded and unknown battlefields and sickbeds, are unforgettable to God. He honors offerings made with all one's might, regardless of who else may notice. So when our turn comes, let us do the job with all our might until the season ends, our understanding is full, and the places of our work are holy.

If ye labor with all your might, I will consecrate that spot that it shall be made holy.[4]

But just what is the work of the sufferer? Is there really a mission for one whose limbs are immovable, whose strength is gone, or whose mind is nearly expended by gnawing pain? To those in tribulation, the Lord has given special goals: faithfulness, patience, and cheer. It's all inner work.[5]

Because thou hast done this with such unwearyingness, behold, I will bless thee forever.[6]

On the other hand, to endure suffering poorly might mean to grow weary. Worn-out faith and endurance fade into despair and bitterness. Of course, God never wears out or faints by the way. For the weary in need of endurance, the Son has said, "Come unto me, all ye that labour and are heavy laden, and I will give you rest."[7]

The Lord, the Creator of the ends of the earth, fainteth not, neither is weary. . . . He giveth power to the faint; and to them that have no might he increaseth strength. . . . They that wait upon the Lord shall renew their strength; . . . they shall run, and not be weary; and they shall walk, and not faint.[8]

We are not here to wait out our troubles with grit and guts but to work through them with grace and goodness. In our suffering, some work opportunities close, but others open as never before.

Notes

1. Moroni 9:6.
2. Ecclesiastes 9:10.
3. Luke 2:52; D&C 93:12–14.
4. D&C 124:44.
5. D&C 54:10; 58:2; John 16:33.
6. Helaman 10:5.
7. Matthew 11:28.
8. Isaiah 40:28–29, 31.

14

Faith Fullness

From the Fall, we inherit disease and disability, indignity and insecurity, muddle and mishap. Christ's work is to sweep away these inherited problems. Our work is to react to them with faith. Meanwhile, circumstances test our confidence in Christ's ability to help us.

Faith is the perfect policy. It was Joseph Smith's policy long before his descent into Liberty dungeon, and once Joseph was there the Lord simply urged him to keep it up: "Hold on thy way."[1] Joseph was to stay true to what he knew. We too can react in Joseph's "way" to our mortal situation—the way of the faithful. To be loyal, we hold firmly to the rod no matter what bumps into us from the left or the right.

To handle the heaviest weight, a weight lifter needs good form. For example, the notorious backsquat measures overall strength but is just plain uncomfortable. With the loaded bar across his shoulders, the lifter descends very low and rises again to a standing position. Good form consists in keeping chest full, spine straight, head up, speed steady, balance perfect, and feet firmly planted.

This reminds us of the spiritual realm. In fact, the word *suffer* literally means to bear or carry from underneath—to "undergo."[2] Under the heaviest weight, we do not feel like being true to our training. Graceful as good form may be, it does not feel graceful at the time! But good form is not just more graceful, it is more powerful. Holding true to our sacred knowledge is not just a tidy way to pass through the fire; it is the only way through.

For our faith to be measured, we must pass through trials that offer no sight of deliverance. Satan hopes we will despair and give up on God. He hopes we will let go of what we know. If our faith is strong only under small loads, it is not fully grown. If we have confidence in God only during the good times, we are foolish.

Then Job . . . fell down upon the ground, and worshipped, and said, . . . the Lord gave, and the Lord hath taken away; blessed be the name of the Lord. In all this Job sinned not, nor charged God foolishly.[3]

Faith in the full degree does not foolishly accuse God. It insists on his goodness, wisdom, and power. It is tenacious and firm. A fullness of faith knows that suffering somehow makes sense, that God must disguise his hand during our little probation, that suffering is a fleeting detail in eternity, and that someday we will see the big map that explains the path we were treading.

The faithful know that doubt can cancel joy but pain cannot. The faithful keep good form. They keep the fire of faith alive by remembering the living Christ and living for him.[4]

May not the things which I have written grieve thee, to weigh thee down unto death; but may Christ lift thee up, and may his sufferings and death, and the showing his body unto our fathers, and his mercy and long-suffering, and the hope of his glory and of eternal life, rest in your mind forever.[5]

But what if, under the weight of heavy trouble, we have sometimes complained, despaired, forgotten the Lord, or even charged him foolishly? (To ask these questions is itself an act of faith — a good sign). For the lifter who drops the bar, the prescription is simple: more training. Strength will grow as we work on good form.

They did press their way forward, continually holding fast to the rod of iron, until they came forth and fell down and partook of the fruit of the tree.[6]

After urging Joseph to hold on his way, the Lord promised, "God shall be with you forever and ever."[7] For a mind full of faith, that settles everything.

Notes

1. D&C 122:9.
2. *Noah Webster's First Edition*, s.v. "Suffer."
3. Job 1:20–22.
4. Job 13:15; 27:5.
5. Moroni 9:25.
6. 1 Nephi 8:30.
7. D&C 122:9.

15

Calm at the Core

Time glides along when life makes sense. But a mind full of doubt can see no plot in a story filled with setbacks, pain, and loneliness. When the story slows down, so does time. But faith sees drama in the trauma. It knows how the story will go and never has to stop believing in the eventual happy ending. When faith says there is purpose in temporary things, it breathes hope back into the story and restores the plot, knowing that the universe ticks warmly in the background of our adventures. Faith gives us patience.

The patience of faith is called long-suffering. Is it painful? No, quite the opposite. Because patience invites meaning, dignity, and the companionship of heaven, it relieves pain of mind. It enables us to last. Real patience really is patient—no fidgeting, no frustration beneath the surface, no pacing back and forth. Patience does not mind waiting. It bends meekly before the necessary and stands firm before the unnecessary, never cowering or pouting. It inherits the earth. Nothing quite compares to the rest and freedom of a life lived in patient faith.

Time grips only those who fear it. Because we have to live within time to transcend it, the patient person adopts the honest and eternal as a clock, which slows down or speeds up as needed to keep pace with God. (Have you noticed that we sometimes like to get ahead of him?) It is the right pace, not speed, that creates a good story and parts the veil.

So great was their faith and their patience that the voice of the Lord came unto them.[1]

The patience of faith is based on gospel hope, which in turn is based on gospel truth. Knowing all things, God abounds with hope. If we cannot know all that he knows, we can still trust what he knows and hope with him.[2]

It helps us to adopt patient heroes. For example, our first parents tamed the earth and ministered to their family for nine centuries—a long time to keep trusting the story! History is full of serene heroes, including the ones all around us right now who show how the story goes, how it polishes, and how it turns out. From them we get a calm perspective.[3]

In all his roles, such as creating temporal things or perfecting eternal things, the God of patience is joyous and calm to the core. The Son is likewise patient in his sensitive and endless work of redemption. In remembrance of their patient gifts, we can give a soft answer, give up a soft chair, give our best, or give our life.

This thing is a similitude of the sacrifice of the Only Begotten of the Father.[4]

Willing offerings put us in good company. Consent makes an offering acceptable. It gives meaning to our story and sense to our suffering. To suffer in remembrance of Christ, to replace whim of self with the will of God, makes sense. On the other hand, the unwilling sufferer seems caught in a pointless plot, a restless story that lacks sense. If the Only Begotten is forgotten, our suffering may not make so much sense after all.

> *But let patience have her perfect work, that ye may be perfect and entire, wanting nothing.*[5]

Especially in the part of the story where everything is at stake, the hero should be patient. That part is now.

Notes

1. Mosiah 24:16.
2. Alma 34:41.
3. James 5:10.
4. Moses 5:7.
5. James 1:4.

16

Be of Good Cheer

Cheer and gloom come from opposite sources. If we must suffer, we might as well be of good cheer. To the ancient self within, things make more sense that way. The blue sky of the great plan, obscured by despair, is unveiled by good cheer.

> *Things will work out. If you keep trying and praying and working, things will work out. They always do.[1]*

Good cheer is modest, bright, and sincere. It is good. It does not capitalize on misfortune to gain sympathy. It bathes trouble in a warm, unselfish light. In good cheer there is no darkness. Good cheer works and worships rather than worries; it shares peace and soothes hearts rather than spreads pain. It stirs the suffering mind with the fresh air of hope and certainty.[2]

> *Latter-day Saints . . . should not suffer reverses and unpleasant circumstances to sour their natures and render them fretful and unsocial . . . , creating gloom and sorrow in their habitations, making themselves feared rather than beloved.[3]*

We respond to good cheer in this world because of our long history with light in the life before. Thus, children naturally believe that things will be okay. But anxiety, the denial of light, erodes our original cheery nature. Pain invites us to doubt the "okay" approach to things. If we accept that invitation, a chain of anxieties will follow.

Hope deferred maketh the heart sick.[4]

One anxiety in that chain is the fear of further pain: "How long will this last?" An even more terrifying and misleading link is, "This wasn't supposed to happen." Our fond plans seem holy to us, as if they were the very plans of God. Timid doubt thinks perhaps God himself has lost control. And yet another anxiety may erupt: "No one cares." Self-centered, self-deceiving, and self-defeating, anxiety robs us of good cheer and chains us to a dungeon floor.

Fear none of those things which thou shalt suffer.[5]

The truth is, our troubles are not so mighty when viewed from eternity. We preceded the world and will long outlive it. We can ignore its passing threats, smile at its thorns, and enjoy its good things.[6]

The good things which come of the earth . . . are made for the benefit and the use of man, both to please the eye and to gladden the heart; . . . for taste and for smell, to strengthen the body and to enliven the soul.[7]

Good cheer, so basic to our nature, is kindled by increasing the other "goods" in life. Let surroundings be flavored with good music and natural beauty, with good tastes and smells. Let words and works be unselfish. Let associations be with others of good cheer. Believe the good promises of God. These things remind us of our home of light.

> *In the world ye shall have tribulation: but be of good cheer; I have overcome the world.*[8]

Stunning blows to the life of a good soul are normal and should be expected. But from him who overcame all things we have a commandment to be of good cheer. It is our way of overcoming *with* him.[9]

Notes

1. Gordon B. Hinckley, in Sheri L. Dew, *Go Forward with Faith*, 423.
2. D&C 68:6.
3. Brigham Young, *Journal of Discourses*, 11:136.
4. Proverbs 13:12.
5. Revelation 2:10.
6. 2 Timothy 1:7.
7. D&C 59:17–19.
8. John 16:33.
9. D&C 61:36.

17

The Second Yes

If affliction calls into question our friendship with God, then affliction is an opportunity to answer that question with faith. It is easy to say "yes" to discipleship in well-lit chapels and in good health. But, as in getting married, the first yes launches a long relationship filled with opportunities to say yes again. We repeatedly confirm our loyalty until there can be no question.

The faith necessary unto the enjoyment of life and salvation never could be obtained without the sacrifice of all earthly things.[1]

The second yes, confirming the first, is not usually spoken in words. But however spoken, the demanding language of loyalty makes clear what and whom we love.[2]

Nephi spoke his famous words, "I will go and do," in the light of his father's tent.[3] But these words led him to a darkened Jerusalem street, where a second yes required that he use Laban's sword. This was but one of many cycles that welded Nephi to his God.

On the road to Damascus, Paul asked, "Lord, what wilt thou have me to do?"[4] Paul's rather uncomplicated yes to the Lord's answer was only the beginning. Each challenging cycle that followed called for a second yes by which Paul could verify his loyalty.

When a pioneer woman diligently pulled her cart up yet another hill, she was saying yes again, verifying former decisions. Her second yes was all the more convincing and audible to the hosts of heaven.

All among them who . . . are willing to observe their covenants by sacrifice — yea, every sacrifice which I, the Lord, shall command — they are accepted of me.[5]

This eloquent language applies mostly to mortals. Premortals and post-mortals can speak of priorities, but from the dark, sheer canyons of the second estate we state our devotion with extra clarity. The suffering mortal soul, unheard by other mortals, cries out a testament of allegiance. Immortals stop to listen in reverence. The second yes echoes through eternity. It breathes sense into our suffering.

We will fully understand the language of loyalty only after our mortal schooling. We will remember its difficult phrases and courageous messages. We will forever honor those who spoke it well. But our gift to speak the quiet grammar of faith, the rich dialect of cheer, and the sweet poetry of patience will be lost when we leave this mortal scene. If we do not make statements clearly in that language while it is our turn to do so, we will forever wish we had. This is our last chance.

God accepts the early yes, the one that gets things started. But the latter yes, uttered in discomfort, is the convincing one. Our second yes and the ones that follow will stand forever as monuments to our lives. Perhaps they are the only things we came here to say.

Notes

1. Joseph Smith, *Lectures on Faith*, 6:58.
2. D&C 136:31.
3. 1 Nephi 3:7.
4. Acts 9:6.
5. D&C 97:8.

18
"In the Day of Adversity Consider"

How easy it is to falsely measure our fortunes. When we have more money, health, honor, or pleasure, are we winning? Not necessarily, for our ills and fortunes are tests, not grades.

> *And he began to teach them, that the Son of man must suffer many things. . . .*
> *And Peter took him, and began to rebuke him. But . . . he rebuked Peter, saying,*
> *. . . Thou savourest not the things that be of God, but the things that be of men.*[1]

Even the chief apostle, Peter, early in his growth, found it hard to savor or value what was best. To savor the wrong things guarantees unhappiness. Suffering is a time to reeducate our hopes, our savoring reflexes. It offers us an elevated spot above the landscape, a rare view, a chance at real wisdom.

But haste and self-pity can deny us the solemn and sweet fruit of wisdom, just when it is ripe. In haste, we forget to reflect. In self-pity, we ask the wrong questions.

> *To ask, Why does this have to happen to me? . . . will lead you into blind alleys.*
> *. . . Rather ask, What am I to do? What am I to learn from this experience?*
> *What am I to change? Whom am I to help?*[2]

To learn from adversity, we need to slow down, kneel down, listen carefully, and consult the sacred books. We can even make our own sacred record, a book of remembrances and reflections. We can consider the suffering of those around us. We can think about him who bore all burdens.[3]

In the day of adversity consider.[4]

If we consider well, without haste and self-pity, the Father's mind will at length whisper to ours. We will see past the outward. We will be settled, even in the smallest holdings and poorest fortunes. We will know that an outward loss opens the door to inner gain.[5]

The emergency in your life may invite my life into action. You will then be like the blind man who helped others to see.[6] If we consider well, we may see the mission in our submission.

Take my yoke upon you, and learn of me.[7]

Not far from our life's lessons is the Teacher. We endure his lessons well by considering them well, by trusting him, and by living what he teaches.

Notes

1. Mark 8:31–33.
2. Richard G. Scott, "Trust in the Lord," *Ensign*, November 1995, 17.
3. Helaman 3:35.
4. Ecclesiastes 7:14.

5. Psalm 37:16.
6. John 9:3, 39.
7. Matthew 11:29.

19

Dispelling Fear Ahead of Time

Fear is perhaps the worst part of suffering. It is the dread prospect of new agonies, the sense of doom, the horror of no hope. Fear freezes and disfigures. It shrinks one's world to the size of one's pain. It can make a crippled limb into a paralyzed life. But there is a cure for fear. According to eternal law, preparation dispels fear.

If ye are prepared ye shall not fear.[1]

In advance of trials, we can short-circuit the worst part of suffering by neutralizing fear. We prepare for future changes by embracing change in the day of ease. Small trials, if accepted, prepare us for large trials. We prepare to calmly face our death by calmly facing life.

Wherefore gird up the loins of your mind.[2]

The lumbar area of the back, from the lowest ribs to the top of the hips, is known as the loins. During heavy labor, this region of muscle becomes fatigued. The spine becomes a yielding hinge instead of a firm column. Throughout history, in battle or harvest, people have learned to wrap or gird this area of the body with extra support. Just when strength is needed, the mind too can wear out, infecting the heart in turn. To gird up the loins of the mind is to get a healthy view—a fearless view—of coming burdens. From God's mind we can borrow spine for the season of suffering. A firm mind braces the heart.[3]

> *Put upon thy servants the testimony of the covenant, . . . that thy people may not faint in the day of trouble.[4]*

Those who have no dealings with God are prone to faint in the day of trouble. Like seeds in shallow soil, they wither under the heat of tribulation because they have no root. We do not acquire deep roots at the last minute. We may rush the lecture but not the lab. We need both in our preparations against fear.

Are we like Martha, "careful and troubled about many things"?[5] Are we too careful about successes that cannot really help? Are we too troubled over failures that cannot really hurt? If so, we are planted in shallow soil, and tomorrow's hot sun may scorch rather than enlighten.[6]

> *There is no fear in love; but perfect love casteth out fear.[7]*

The murky waters of fear boil up from the mud of selfishness. Love and fear exclude each other, so we should not be surprised if generosity is central to the lab we are taking. Long before Job's famous suffering, he had unwittingly prepared himself by private service:

> *I delivered the poor that cried, and the fatherless, and him that had none to help him. The blessing of him that was ready to perish came upon me: and I caused the widow's heart to sing for joy. . . . I was eyes to the blind, and feet was I to the lame. I was a father to the poor.*[8]

Behind the fearless Job is the selfless Job. The preparing present begs us to love truth, life, others—and to do all this loving with energy. Today girds us for tomorrow's growth.

Notes

1. D&C 38:30.
2. 1 Peter 1:13.
3. D&C 58:5; 75:22.
4. D&C 109:38.
5. Luke 10:41.
6. Matthew 13:5–6, 20–21.
7. 1 John 4:18.
8. Job 29:12–13, 15–16.

20

Glimpses of Integrity

The spirits of the just, who had been faithful in the testimony of Jesus while they lived in mortality; and who had offered sacrifice in the similitude of the great sacrifice of the Son of God, and had suffered tribulation in their Redeemer's name.[1]

The suffering of our Savior is in a category by itself. But there is another category, the suffering of his followers. These sufferings are offerings, made to him with integrity and loyalty, as illustrated in the following examples.[2]

From Ann, a victim of childhood abuse:

From age five through fifteen, I was subjected to extreme abuse at the hands of my stepfather. I struggled for years with feelings of great unworthiness. I was quite inactive and bitter as a Church member. My heart became quite hardened. I suppose you could say I was spiritually bruised and broken. I couldn't bring myself to pray to someone in heaven who was supposed to be my father. I rejected priesthood blessings because even the touch of worthy priesthood holders was a threat. I got so lost in my deep, dark place that I got to thinking that life would be better off without me.

But, as I later learned, others were praying for me. On a strange impulse, I accepted the challenge to just do two little things each day for my spirit: read one verse from the Book of Mormon and pray for one minute. Though I was disgusted with myself for agreeing to do this, I kept my word. It may seem like almost nothing to do these two things, but for me they were not easy! I read one verse from some random spot in the book and then stared at the clock in a kneeling position for the remaining minute.

I continued this routine for many weeks before my heart began to soften. A miracle was taking place. One verse became two, then three, and then chapters. A hunger was awakened, and I feasted on the word of the Lord. I found myself praying to my Heavenly Father as I would talk to a friend. He became real. I knew he was listening to me. I knew he was answering my prayers. I came to realize that he cherished me.

I have turned my burdens over to the Lord, and he has included them in his atonement somehow. They are gone. I'm free of the wounds and anger that once haunted me night and day. Twenty-five years of therapy did not do for me what the gospel has done. The Savior is the ultimate therapist and the ultimate healer.

From Lee, afflicted with a rare form of dwarfism:

I am a dwarf whose adult stature is three-foot-ten. However, if mere "shortness" were the sole factor in my affliction, this would be a short story indeed. My condition entails medical complications that have required major surgeries over the years, many of them followed by extended months in a body cast. In this life, I will never know a normal lifestyle, though miracle after miracle has kept me alive and able to function in many ways.

Sometimes our faith might seem to be one of our trials! But it is unbelief that increases our suffering, perhaps a hundredfold. However unbearable my physical and mental pain have been at times, however keen my sense of isolation from normal friendships, and even though it isn't the Lord's pleasure to remove all these problems just now, everything would only be worse without the light of Christ to put things in a clearer perspective.

We suffer most when each moment seems as if it ought to be the last. How have we lasted so long? How do we go on? We shall have to settle on mere glimpses of the eternal plan, for that is all we can or even ought to possess in this life. That makes this life a test of character. I haven't found one big answer to make it more bearable, but I know that the whole gospel plan, put together, keeps me going. I know I have covenanted with the Father to take this journey and return to him. Covenants aren't made with immediate rewards in mind, but he will keep his promises. There is absolutely no reason in the universe why we shouldn't trust him.

There are strained times when I find myself enduring to the end out of a sense of duty, but I would like to do this more out of love. When love starts to seep into our coarse mortal personalities, those are the moments when we are not only passing the test with flying colors but are beginning to realize that the test is just that—a test. We can't call it quits, and we can't peek ahead. It does little good to look at others' tests because every single one is different.

I'm here partly for self-improvement, but that motive somehow doesn't help me very much during the worst moments. I have to remember that I'm here because the Father and Son said it was the best thing for me. I take them at their word. I'm here because I love them. The quick road to exaltation probably just leads to a quick detour. Following the example set by Jesus, I'm willing to work from the bottom up.

From Scott, recovering from back surgery and remembering his friend Dave, who died of cancer:

As I lie here in quite a lot of pain, confined to this terrible prison of a reclining chair, I wonder at the millions who endure worse. They travel the same mental deserts of pounding pain. Dave did. And there are so many Daves.

Before the diagnosis, Dave was a budding scientist in his mid-twenties doing graduate work at the university. But he passed away this summer after a long struggle with cancer. His trials were so much greater and longer than the ones that tonight seem to be pushing me to the limit of my sanity. The hills on his desert of pain were steeper. And he had to climb each tortuous hill know-ing that what was coming next would be even worse.

I remember one of my last visits with him. The racking pain had become constant. The battle had already been long. His patience had been stretched beyond anything he and Jennifer had expected. I recall looking down into his face while kneeling at the side of his cot. We were about to pray together. He wanted us to ask Heavenly Father to take him home.

"Have I grown enough? Can I go now? Am I finished?" he asked.

"Almost enough," seemed to be the Lord's answer.

After a few more days of superhuman fortitude, the miracle came. Dave's body released him into the spirit realm. No more stabbing pain, horrid nau-sea, dreary aching, or dark delirium. But I suppose he will always have the patience he gained during that last year or two of his life—a kind of eternal trophy from a marathon.

And up until the end, Dave spoke of the goodness of God. He could feel it strongly. Was God being good to Dave? If you had asked him then, he would have quietly said that God was with him and would soon take him into his arms. I imagine that if we could speak with Dave now, he could tell us even more about the goodness of God.

From Tammy (currently a stake Relief Society president), who spent years in depression linked to a debilitating illness:

I was energetic and healthy until twelve years ago, when I seemed to become one of the living dead. I found myself consumed with fatigue and depression. In my few waking, coherent moments, I felt I was struggling for survival. I was diagnosed with CFS (chronic fatigue syndrome). Involuntarily, I had been thrust as a helpless combatant into a war I didn't understand and had no hope of winning.

Physically I was in ruins. I felt as if I were encased in a concrete body cast, just concentrating on literally putting one foot in front of the other. I had to safeguard my energies and learn to say "no." People who knew the previous me were surprised. My mind became dull and unresponsive. I could remember nothing. I was lost in a place deep and despairing, and I wondered about the fine line between sanity and insanity. I felt I would cross it and never return if I gave up my feeble attempts to stay sane.

Emotionally, I was crippled and void. The real me was being replaced by someone I didn't know or like. I felt enslaved, entombed, and helpless. I planned my funeral. I was not a paragon in dealing with suffering, for that took energy I didn't have. I saw myself as a lazy, muddle-headed, irresponsible, unfocused, ', pathetic, weak-willed, sleeping lump of nothingness. And then at some point rage became my constant companion. I felt like a Dr. Jekyll and Mr. Hyde.

How did I react spiritually? I allowed all this to strangle my spirit. Without making the choice, I had chosen not to be refined by this refiner's opportunity. It became a hopeless, downward spiral from which I saw no escape. I lived in the shadows, and it was simply easier to erode. I became cynical. I had constructed a nice, neat, private prison within my own mind into which I withdrew and secluded myself. I'd forgotten where to find the solution. I am ashamed to say it, and even now writing it brings tears to my eyes, but my rage then turned on my Heavenly Father. I became increasingly bitter and felt unworthy. I was at a dangerous point. I had stopped praying. I had personally removed the armor of God and opened myself to direct assault by the adversary. I had excluded the Spirit from my life.

I'm not sure when the defining moment occurred. I only remember I was having my all-too-familiar conversation with death. At the very moment I asked myself how I would take my life, something buried deep within me, something long dormant, came rushing to the surface, screaming and demanding immediate attention. I was frightened and began to cry. This moment came in answer to the prayers of others on my behalf, for I had not been forgotten. I am forever grateful for their unwavering faith and love. This was my moment of truth, the moment to set aside all of my self-pitying, self-destructive behavior, the moment to live and get on with living. I fell to my knees, asking for help, for strength, for forgiveness. I had remembered the key, the simple key: prayer.

That was when the slow turn began. Praying and studying the Book of Mormon eventually became my lifelines. The sacrament became my time to

*cleanse and unburden, a time of renewal, remembrance, learning, and hope.
Am I a better person for my experiences? Yes, I am. Will I forget the lessons
learned? No, the journey was too painful. Was I healed physically? No, not in
the way I desired. Do I still struggle? Yes, for this life is about struggles.*

*We are not strong enough to carry the burdens of this life. The plan is
simple. We are the ones who by choice invite the Savior into our life or make
life more difficult than it needs to be by denying him access. He is always there
and we are always loved. When we arm ourselves with spiritual defenses, we
invite the healing and peace of the Atonement into our lives. These principles
are true.*

Notes

1. D&C 138:12–13.
2. Names have been changed.

BENEATH WATCHFUL EYES

We need the Lord's truths and doctrines in our sufferings, but we also need him. Each time one of the Father's children opens the confusing gift of growth, wrapped in difficulty, he watches. Under his eye and amid earthly and heavenly loved ones who are learning to be like him, the sufferer is not alone.

Beneath his watchful eye, his Saints securely dwell (*Hymns*, no. 125).

Furthermore, the sufferer often opens the gift in the presence of earthly friends. As one of those friends, you or I sometimes have the privilege of joining the Father in his watch care.

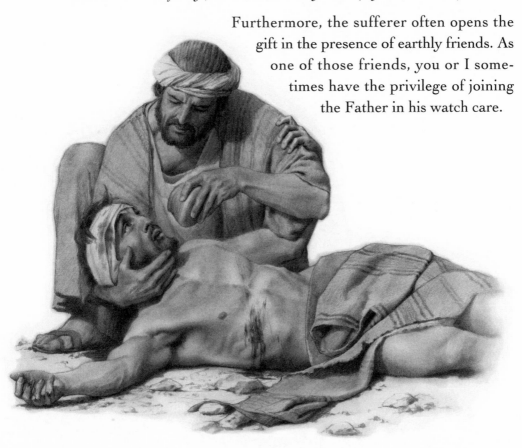

21

The Worth and Joy of Souls

We cannot comprehend the value of a soul, not even our own. In our Father's eyes, we are literally worth everything, so the calculations are quite beyond us.

Our worth is connected with our purpose, which was settled long before our birth into this world. Just what is the aim of our existence? Very simply, it is joy.

Men are, that they might have joy.[1]

Our worth is related to our potential for everlasting happiness. It is a big mistake to assign worth to one's self or another based on anything less, such as earthly possessions or positions. Joy in the private experience of a soul is the one treasure that must not be neglected and cannot be replaced. No wonder a soul is of greater worth than the combined value of all things in this world or in millions of worlds like it. Things do not experience joy, so they do not have inherent worth.

No man can conceive how great is the worth of souls. One soul saved which would have been lost means added kingdoms and worlds, added spirit children born to exalted beings, added hosts of intelligent beings going forward ever-lastingly in eternal progression.[2]

Lasting joy does not grow out of recreation, humor, or even health. Lasting joy and great glory result from complying with law.[3] Joy at the core of our private experience is only possible if we are following our conscience. If our conscience or our integrity is diminished, so is our happiness. The ultimate tragedy is an undeveloped, unrealized capacity for joy. To help someone break out of a joyless prison is the ultimate mission.

The saved individual is the supreme end of the divine will.[4]

For this reason the Father and the Son are determined to carry out their astonishing, gracious plan of happiness and to raise each of us to a higher platform for joy.

Remember the worth of souls is great in the sight of God; for, behold, the Lord your Redeemer suffered death in the flesh; wherefore he suffered the pain of all men, that all men might repent and come unto him.[5]

Because our Father persists in helping his children grow, we should remember what our growth is all about: the capacity for joy. It is no accident that we are invited to join in helping. The work of raising and redeeming others is the purpose of our design, the guarantee of our joy. We are like our Father, finding our fullest satisfaction in the same way he finds his.[6]

Notes

1. 2 Nephi 2:25.
2. Bruce R. McConkie, *Doctrinal New Testament Commentary,* 3:46.
3. D&C 88:20–24, 38–39; Alma 41:10–14.
4. David O. McKay, "Man . . . the Jewel of God," *Improvement Era,* December 1969, 31.
5. D&C 18:10–11.
6. D&C 18:15; Alma 31:35.

22

The Pains of All Men

Some have falsely accused God of permitting the "combined suffering" of all mankind. But how could suffering be combined? Our experiences, painful or pleasant, are personal. Sensation is limited to the individual. What happens in the seclusion of one soul cannot be joined with what happens in the seclusion of another soul.

For example, suppose you and I each get a bump on the head. Let us say that we each suffer about fifty units of pain. Does this somehow add up to one hundred units of pain? No, because the sensation of a bumped head is private. Your fifty units cannot be added to my fifty units in the way that impersonal things can be added. There is no spot within us or outside us where our separate pains can merge. We feel our bumps privately, even if we got them by running into each other!

Of course, a friend may see us run into each other and be seized with his own fifty units of anxiety just because he cares so much. But his anxious mind is his alone. Meanwhile, none of us is in on the experience of another friend suffering next door with an earache. That makes four of us, and we have not even left the neighborhood yet. But the suffering is not mixed together at all.

What is private for the four of us is private for a million of us—a million private worlds, each one insulated from all others.

It dehumanizes the souls of mankind to think that this solemn business of trauma can be combined as one might mix a dozen eggs in a bowl. God should not be blamed for a combined mass of suffering.

But now we must reverently note an exception to this: God comprehends all. He knows our experience in multiples not only of two or four but also in multiples of millions and billions. In one eternal "now,"[1] he knows every bumped head, every earache, every hurt, and every horror.

He suffereth the pains of all men, yea, the pains of every living creature, both men, women, and children, who belong to the family of Adam.[2]

The Father comprehended the ordeal of his Son, and the members of the Godhead ordained that the infinite burden of combined suffering be theirs alone. With that magnificent exception, there is no combined suffering in the universe or the world. One nightmare at a time is as bad as it gets. No heartless multiplier exists out there, permitting a combined suffering.

The arithmetic of anguish is something we mortals cannot comprehend.[3]

Rather than accuse, let critics worship the Watcher and Empathizer, who permits only a confined suffering for each of us and who took upon himself the pains of all.

He shall go forth, suffering pains and afflictions and temptations of every kind; . . . he will take upon him the pains and the sicknesses of his people. And he will take upon him death, . . . and he will take upon him their infirmities, that his bowels may be filled with mercy, according to the flesh, that he may know according to the flesh how to succor his people according to their infirmities.[4]

Notes

1. Joseph Smith, *Teachings of the Prophet Joseph Smith*, 220.
2. 2 Nephi 9:21.
3. Neal A. Maxwell, *All These Things Shall Give Thee Experience*, 37.
4. Alma 7:11–12.

23

He Chastens

Under his watchful eye we are *chastened*. The meaning of this interesting word is to discipline, purify, prune, refine, humble, subdue. Thus, our Father's chastening is not a prison but a passage to his presence — not a forbidding wall but an inviting veil.

Whom I love I also chasten.[1]

Since it is he who loves us, it is he who chastens us. Who, then, will not be chastened at some time?[2]

I have borne chastisement, I will not offend any more.[3]

God's chastening might be thought of as a bridge arching upward. It is not a popular route, of course, for it rises away from the customary and comfortable. But it is heaven bound and sometimes the only way home.[4]

How much better it would be for the Lord to chasten us . . . than to suffer us to live in carelessness.[5]

His chastening alters us, as the stone made precious by the agonies of nature or as gold refined by excruciating heat. What only glittered with possibility before is made glorious after. Pure gold is sometimes a symbol for the celestial, but it is just a symbol. The purified life is the real thing. And the Great Refiner personally supervises our transformation.[6]

> *Constant, intense pain is a great consecrating purifier that humbles us and draws us closer to God's Spirit.*[7]

This chastening washes out stubborn stains. The Father whispers to the squirmy child, "Now, now. Hold still. You want to be clean, don't you?" Washing precedes anointing; deep cleaning prepares for inpouring light. Is there a washing before the anointing of the sick and afflicted? Perhaps the affliction itself is the washing. Perhaps the salty tears and sweat of sorrow are tokens of the sacred inner process of becoming clean.[8]

> *If I wash thee not, thou hast no part with me.*[9]

With his chastening hand, he wakens the drowsy. If we are too busy and petty, if lesser things have outgrown greater things, urgency will rescue us. The clanging alarm neither harms nor interrupts. It just gets us back on schedule, quickens the heart, and pierces our air of self-sufficiency. Even the sound of our own crying reminds us that we are children after all.

> *He hath spoken unto you in a still small voice, but ye were past feeling, that*

ye could not feel his words; wherefore, he has spoken unto you like unto the voice of thunder.[10]

His chastening hand reaches out to separate us from our lower tendencies; to make us extraordinary; to purify, wash, and waken us; and to lead us home. It topples egos and reduces options so that we will not waste precious time. It draws our attention to the only one who solves real problems.[11] On closer inspection, we will see that this hand has suffered chastisement on our behalf[12] and that it was the hand of fellowship all along.

Notes

1. D&C 95:1.
2. D&C 136:31; Deuteronomy 8:5; Hebrews 12:5–7, 9–11.
3. Job 34:31.
4. Helaman 3:29–30.
5. Orson Pratt, *Journal of Discourses*, 3:297.
6. 1 Peter 1:7; Malachi 3:3; John 15:1–3.
7. Robert D. Hales, "The Covenant of Baptism: To Be in the Kingdom and of the Kingdom," *Ensign*, November 2000, 6.
8. D&C 90:36.
9. John 13:8.
10. 1 Nephi 17:45.
11. Helaman 12:3; Job 23:16.
12. Isaiah 53:5.

24

He Delivers

God prefers to relieve our suffering, and circumstances often permit him to do so. In fact, the scriptures speak much on the sweet subject of deliverance.

> *I, Nephi, will show unto you that the tender mercies of the Lord are over all those whom he hath chosen, because of their faith, to make them mighty even unto the power of deliverance.*[1]

The subject of deliverance is a golden thread appearing throughout the golden plates. Consider how often *deliver* and *delivered* appear in the Book of Mormon. The thread of deliverance also appears on many pages of our hymnal and even in the hymnbook of times past, the Psalms.

> *Many are the afflictions of the righteous: but the Lord delivereth him out of them all.*[2]

Yes, deliverance implies that we will have trouble. But the promise remains that we will be "supported under trials and troubles of every kind, yea, and in all manner of afflictions"[3] to the degree that we put our trust in God.[4] To be supported means that God will add his power to ours.

In trials—when we are tested for faithfulness—he will protect us from our weaknesses. In troubles—when things are breaking down, falling apart, and going out of control—he will calm us. In afflictions—when we suffer acute pain of mind or body—he will bless us by removing the pain or giving us power to endure it.

My God hath been my support.[5]

The Hebrew name *Joshua* or *Jeshua* (from which we get *Jesus*) means "God is help" or "Savior."[6] Our Father really is our help, and his aid comes to us through Jesus.[7] The Atonement makes divine deliverance possible. It allows God to intervene in the imperfect life, heal what he cannot condone, and subdue those very forces that caused the Savior to suffer. Because of the Atonement, God's own work is to renew and rescue, support and save. He never forgets his work of deliverance, is never bored, and never works carelessly.

I am with you to bless you and deliver you forever.[8]

"We have nothing to fear," said President Gordon B. Hinckley, for "God is at the helm."[9] His power to bless is unmatched in all the universe.[10] Far greater than the paltry forces of depression and destruction are his powers to create, lift, and exalt. We can trust that he can easily bless us. Else why would he ask, "Is there any thing too hard for me?"[11]

Notes

1. 1 Nephi 1:20.
2. Psalm 34:19.
3. Alma 36:27.
4. Alma 36:3; 38:5.
5. 2 Nephi 4:20.
6. Bible Dictionary, s.v. "Jesus."
7. Moroni 7:22.
8. D&C 108:8.
9. Gordon B. Hinckley, "This Is the Work of the Master," *Ensign,* May 1995, 71.
10. Romans 8:31.
11. Jeremiah 32:27.

25

Guiding Us to Plan A

Facing a major loss, one faithful man asked, "So is that the end of plan A?" In other words, had the Lord for some reason canceled the main event, the highest blessings? Of course not. Our Father leads us into valleys, but ahead of us are even greater elevations than we have known before. The greatest days are yet to come. With each passing mile, plan A gets closer all the time.

What is man . . . that thou shouldest set thine heart upon him? And . . . visit him every morning, and try him every moment?[1]

Job, for one, may have felt God had too many plans for him! Why all this close trying and training, and all the starting over again? God was not following Job's plan, he was changing Job into a grand and holy being! He placed Job below the angels and monitored him incessantly. God's attention to us comes not from too little love for us but from what C. S. Lewis called "the intolerable compliment of loving us, in the deepest, most tragic, most inexorable sense."[2]

Fear thou not; for I am with thee: be not dismayed; for I am thy God: I will strengthen thee; yea, I will help thee; yea, I will uphold thee with the right hand of my righteousness.[3]

Before we accomplish plan A, we face ironies—humble preliminaries that seem unrelated to the main event. In the tedious cultivation, in the rambling route of agency, in the time-consuming preparations, even the faithful seldom notice God's hand moving them toward plan A. Jesus himself had to descend before ascending. Surely we are no greater than he.[4]

He raiseth up the poor . . . to set them among princes, . . . to make them inherit the throne of glory.[5]

But later comes the good kind of irony: wondrous reversals. Plan A, the main event, emerges. For example, countless people have gone through a whole mortal existence without basic blessings—health, sanity, happiness, parents, spouse, children—or have lost them along the way. But there awaits, perhaps in the world of spirits, a stunning harvest after all that hoping and hoeing, thanks to the God of perfect reversals.[6]

Thy right hand hath holden me up, and thy gentleness hath made me great.[7]

Timing is everything. God unfolds his deliverance in customized ways that a less comprehending being could never attempt.[8]

Each trial in life is tailored to the individual's capacities and needs.[9]

We need more, not less, irony in our diets. We need God's careful planning, his watchful eye, his miraculous tailoring of our trials. Whatever other crying we do, we must cry unto him for all our support.[10] With that support, we will see the puzzle come together and the main event at last unfold. We are each getting closer, even now.

Notes

1. Job 7:17–18.
2. C. S. Lewis, *The Problem of Pain*, 41.
3. Isaiah 41:10.
4. D&C 122:8.
5. 1 Samuel 2:8.
6. Isaiah 54:1, 7–8; James 5:10; D&C 121:25, 29.
7. Psalm 18:35.
8. D&C 88:58–60.
9. Howard W. Hunter, "Come Unto Me," *Ensign*, November 1990, 18.
10. Alma 37:36; 2 Nephi 32:9.

26

Surrounded by Angels

In the story of Job, we read about an unseen "hedge" or wall defending him from Satan. Evidently, the hedge shields every righteous person, lowered only rarely as the Lord sees fit.[1] This protection reminds us of the heavenly companions he has promised.

> *I will go before your face. I will be on your right hand and on your left, and my Spirit shall be in your hearts, and mine angels round about you, to bear you up.*[2]

We need all the help we can get. "Without me ye can do nothing," said Jesus.[3] Or, as Mormon put it, without miracles and the ministering of angels, which cease because of unbelief, "all is vain."[4] Our need for spiritual succor will persist "so long as time shall last"[5]—so long as we work under the severe conditions of a mortal body, a mortal brain, and a mortal world.

> *Dearest children, holy angels watch your actions night and day.*[6]

Our heavenly associates "think it not beneath their state to abide in the hovels of the poor, to stand by us in the most menial labor."[7] They know of our amnesia and our trouble focusing on important things. To them, we are both needy and precious—the perfect project. Bundled with our joy is theirs. We get some idea of this when it is our privilege to watch over others: our affection increases, their needs occupy our minds, and we want to do for them what they cannot do for themselves.

> *You cannot tell the interest felt in eternity for you, my brethren and sisters, by those of our dead who have gone before us. Their hearts yearn after us.*[8]

So why do they not intervene more often in our suffering? Intervening may be interfering, if it interrupts growth, and this they cannot do. The more clearly we understand the great plan of growth and enlargement of souls, the more we understand their restraint. But they do intervene in certain ways. They "come down and join hand in hand" in our labors.[9] They point our minds to the truth. They encourage our repentance.

> *He is near by, His angels are our associates, they are with us and round about us, and watch over us, and take care of us, and lead us, and guide us, and administer to our wants in their ministry.*[10]

By ourselves, we are small and generate only modest force. But we have the privilege of aligning ourselves with the powers of heaven.[11]

> *Fear not: for they that be with us are more than they that be with them.*[12]

Chief among these giants are the Father and the Son, the ultimate companions. Through the priceless gift of the Holy Ghost, these two Supreme Beings will be close to us "unto the end of the world."[13] They join the angels in rejoicing over our integrity, and along with all the heavenly hosts, their watchful eyes weep over our suffering, sorrow, and sin.[14]

Notes

1. Job 1:10, 12; 2:6; D&C 122:9.
2. D&C 84:88.
3. John 15:5.
4. Moroni 7:37.
5. Moroni 7:36.
6. *Hymns,* no. 96.
7. James E. Talmage, in Stuy, *Collected Discourses,* 3:291.
8. George Q. Cannon, *Journal of Discourses,* 22:131.
9. Joseph Smith, *Teachings of the Prophet Joseph Smith,* 159.
10. Heber C. Kimball, *Journal of Discourses,* 2:222.
11. D&C 35:24; 103:20.
12. 2 Kings 6:16.
13. Matthew 28:20.
14. D&C 62:3; 88:2; Moses 7:28–40.

27

His Comfort

A mmon admits that at a certain point in his ministry with his brothers, "our hearts were depressed, and we were about to turn back."[1] So how did they press forward anyway, changing the course of history and blessing untold thousands? At this crucial point, the Lord comforted them. *Comfort* is related to words like fort and fortify, suggesting strength. To comfort someone is to share your strength with them. The Lord comforts us by his power, promises, and presence.

God is the strength of my heart.[2]

His power is a fortress. He knows the exact limits of our strength, something we usually underestimate. He watches the size of our burdens, which we often overestimate. When the load is too great, he yokes us to himself.[3] By adding his strength to ours, he makes our work feasible, and he honors us by his personal involvement.[4]

For thou hast been a strength to the poor, a strength to the needy in his distress, a refuge from the storm, a shadow from the heat, when the blast of the terrible ones is as a storm against the wall.[5]

His promises offer us a secure place in the fortress. When we hold to the promises with a firm mind, we are more inclined to endure.[6] Nephi, the son of Helaman, pressed on and on because he believed in the Lord's assurances.[7] His "unwearyingness,"[8] in turn, prompted the Lord to make even greater promises to him.[9] So it has always been. Promises anchor the soul.

> *Having this promise sealed unto them, it was an anchor to the soul, sure and steadfast. . . . This hope and knowledge would support the soul in every hour of trial, trouble and tribulation.*[10]

In the heart of the fortress, the presence of the Lord may be found. Our pain opens a door to his chambers, where he quietly waits. But we are not forced to enter. We can remain alone, doubting, self-absorbed, restless. Still, he hopes we will come in. Should we do so, he will stand in the sincerest courtesy as we enter, and he will watch with unwavering attention and affection during our dark and painful hour.

> *I, the Lord God, do visit my people in their afflictions.*[11]

In the fortress of his comfort we may have fellowship with him. After our ordeals are ended, the fellowship will continue in mansions he is now preparing.

> *Live clean, keep the commandments of the Lord, pray to Him constantly . . . and then whatever betides you the Lord will be with you and nothing will*

happen to you that will not be to the honor and glory of God and to your sal-vation and exaltation. There will come into your hearts from the living of the pure life you pray for, a joy that will pass your powers of expression or under-standing. The Lord will be always near you; He will comfort you; you will feel His presence in the hour of your greatest tribulation; He will guard and protect you to the full extent that accords with His all-wise purpose.[12]

Notes

1. Alma 26:27.
2. Psalm 73:26.
3. Matthew 11:29–30.
4. Deuteronomy 31:8; Isaiah 40:29; Alma 31:32–34; D&C 62:1.
5. Isaiah 25:4.
6. Jacob 3:1–2; Alma 58:10–11.
7. Helaman 5:13–14.
8. Helaman 10:4.
9. Helaman 10:5–7.
10. Joseph Smith, *Teachings of the Prophet Joseph Smith*, 298.
11. Mosiah 24:14.
12. The First Presidency, "The Message of the First Presidency to the Church," *Improvement Era*, May 1942, 349.

28

The Privilege and Price of Friendship

When we are not being Job, it is our turn to be his friends, ministering to the afflicted and distraught. The privilege hallows us, for the place where the sufferer encounters his or her God is holy ground. As friends of Job, we are called to be earthly messengers of divine attention, earthly ministering angels. Ministering is the work of heaven, pure religion.[1]

Inasmuch as they are not the saviors of men, they are as salt that has lost its savor, and is thenceforth good for nothing but to be cast out and trodden under foot of men.[2]

Earth is crying for "saviors of men" who, as salt, preserve and save and flavor. Suffering seems to increase around us day by day, but the laborers are few. If we are not saviors, we are "good for nothing" as far as God's work is concerned. Job knew what it was to have friends who were neither sensitive nor wise, who wanted the privilege without the price.[3]

He will take upon him their infirmities, that his bowels may be filled with

mercy, according to the flesh, that he may know according to the flesh how to
succor his people according to their infirmities.[4]

Part of the price of friendship is to learn from our own suffering. Even the Savior learned this way.[5] With a mild headache or a major heartache, we should notice what it means to be alone in pain and how good it is to have a friend. We should also notice the difference between empty service and real service. If we suffer wisely, we will succor wisely.

The privilege of ministering also demands a doing and giving sort of love, instead of just thinking about doing and giving. "I need to get over there and visit him sometime" does not relieve loneliness. It is not real love until it becomes a cheery visit, a listening ear, a good meal, or even a car wash. Love grows more gracious and godly with experience. With exercise, we get better at lifting sorrows and we find joy in doing so.

With the resources they will have at command, they will fly to the relief of the
stranger; they will pour in oil and wine to the wounded heart of the distressed;
they will dry up the tears of the orphan and make the widow's heart to rejoice.[6]

When we really give, we expect no return. God gives in this manner, not keeping track. My two hands have not grown up until they learn to give his way. Resources go rancid in a dark and sweaty grasp. Possessions that do not bless do not matter. If my money does not serve higher interests, the interest it earns makes no difference.[7]

To mend just one broken heart gives meaning to life. It is not hard. To freely give is sweet release — the only way of doing things that is neither hard nor hardening, neither dark nor darkening, neither poor nor impoverishing.[8] Like doing, giving is both price and privilege.

> *A man filled with the love of God, is not content with blessing his family alone, but ranges through the whole world, anxious to bless the whole human race.*[9]

The price of friendship is pure religion, outside and in — loving not only God's children but also God himself, offering both service and sanctity, being benevolent and believing, paying alms and praying with all the heart, relieving the world's ills while remaining unspotted by the world's evil. The pure love and pure eyes of God are bestowed on the true friend.[10]

Notes

1. James 1:27.
2. D&C 103:10.
3. Job 16:1–5; 42:7.
4. Alma 7:12.
5. Hebrews 5:8.
6. Joseph Smith, *History of the Church*, 4:567.
7. Jacob 2:19.
8. Luke 6:30; 1 John 3:17; Mosiah 4:16.
9. Joseph Smith, *Teachings of the Prophet Joseph Smith*, 174.
10. D&C 121:45; Moroni 7:45–48.

29

Suggestions for the Friends of Job

The men who visited Job seemed to understand just about everything except the heavenly patterns of friendship. Fitting wrong truths to the situation and guessing at the reasons for Job's troubles, they were a bit more like enemies than friends. It was as if they were following the opposite of the golden rule: "Do unto others what you hope no one will ever do to you. In the guise of friendship, discourage and depress. If your brother falls down, kick." As true friends of Job, we can do better.[1]

God hath shewed me that I should not call any man common or unclean.[2]

No good comes of asking why another must suffer. Some of earth's finest have suffered ghastly injustice. Good friends react without assuming guilt. Whether in the privacy of thought, behind the back, or to the face, faultfinding falls below an upright friendship.[3] Rather than blame, we can just get to work serving.

The scriptures mention the need to abase (not debase), or to humble and lower ourselves.[4] If we are on a pedestal, we come down and help others up.

To assist with burdens, we cannot be distant. Heaven's pattern of friendship requires empathy and teamwork.[5]

> *We ought to be cheerful while among the sick. When we are well we ought to live our religion and be faithful in our prayers and when we are sick be jovial and get a fiddle and not be cast down.*[6]

True friends relate to the one peering out of tired eyes and speaking through weakened voice. They see dignity even if it is housed in a failing body shrouded in hospital contraptions. They show respect with clean linen and respectful voices. They soften hard edges with humor, smiles, kind touches, and uplifting news. And when affliction permits no embrace or when humor does not fit the moment, they soothe the heart with the joy of reassurance and acceptance.

> *Be ye all of one mind, having compassion one of another, love as brethren, be pitiful, be courteous.*[7]

Our quiet presence may be the voice of God's greeting. If angels and shepherds had to make clear to all of us his goodwill at the birth of Jesus, might he not use one of us to convey his affection to another of us? Heaven whispers in righteous friendships.[8] A teenage boy explained it this way just before leukemia ended his life: "[Be] reassuring and extra, extra kind when the one you love is sad. When you are very sick, it helps to have someone hold your hand, letting the glowing warmth of their love for you trickle into you."[9]

When persons manifest the least kindness and love to me, O what power it has over my mind, while the opposite course has a tendency to harrow up all the harsh feelings and depress the human mind.[10]

Whom should you or I visit? Jesus gave us the answer: "The least of these my brethren"[11]—the least healthy, the least happy, the least supported, the least likely to walk on their own. In addition to calling on the ill and elderly, we should consider visiting the depressed, the unemployed, the recently bankrupt or bereaved, the unpopular, the displaced. And if we cannot actually share their burden, we can serve a good purpose by staying close. The angel who appeared to Jesus and strengthened him during his agony in Gethsemane[12] gives us, perhaps, the ultimate example of a good purpose served by staying close. That angel's role was limited but ever so sacred and appreciated!

He hath sent me to bind up the brokenhearted, . . . to comfort all that mourn.[13]

Often there is no remedy at hand, no quick solution by word or deed. Only passing time, mighty prayer, and redoubled love can help. Words, if needed at all, can be simple. Modest, inspired words can often heal "the wounded soul."[14]

Under the blows of mortal reproof, those who suffer need reassurance, above all, that they are still cherished,[15] that their best patience and faith is all the Lord asks for now, and that their life still has perfect purpose and promise.[16]

> *Succor the weak, lift up the hands which hang down, and strengthen the feeble knees.*[17]

The original meaning of *succor* is to run or dash to someone's aid. How soon we go, how easily we drop everything to help, says something about our esteem for the person in need. Zeal sends one message; hesitation sends another.[18] The best time and most eloquent way to succor is to do so when need arises.[19] After all, service is seldom convenient.

> *Whosoever will be great among you, shall be your minister: and whosoever of you will be the chiefest, shall be servant of all.*[20]

How peculiar it is that real greatness has so much to do with suffering— our own or that of our friends. Christ said, "Ye have done it unto me."[21] He takes our reaction to Job personally, for he himself was Job's best friend.[22]

Notes

1. Job 42:7; Matthew 7:12.
2. Acts 10:28.
3. D&C 88:124.

4. Alma 4:13; D&C 112:3.

5. Romans 12:16; Galatians 6:2; Mosiah 18:8–9.

6. Brigham Young, in *Wilford Woodruff's Journal*, 6:44; punctuation modernized.

7. 1 Peter 3:8.

8. Alma 15:18.

9. Elaine Ipswitch, "Maybe My Time Is Up," *Reader's Digest*, September 1979, 151.

10. Joseph Smith, *Teachings of the Prophet Joseph Smith*, 240.

11. Matthew 25:40.

12. Luke 22:43.

13. Isaiah 61:1–2.

14. Jacob 2:8; Alma 37:8–10.

15. D&C 121:43.

16. Isaiah 35:3.

17. D&C 81:5.

18. Alma 60:6.

19. Matthew 10:42.

20. Mark 10:43–44.

21. Matthew 25:40.

22. Job 19:25–26; 42:12.

30

Glimpses of Grace

The God of heaven looked upon the residue of the people, and he wept; and Enoch bore record of it.[1]

As our Father beholds the expanse of agony and sorrow, he focuses on each broken heart personally. He also discerns the best timing for comfort and relief. He arranges to have friends, mortal and heavenly, gathered around each drama of suffering in an attendant drama of support. Here are some glimpses of his grace.

A ward member visits Vic[2] in the hospital:

> *Vic is just recovering from major surgery in which they discovered a malignant tumor. He's ninety-three, so a lot of us would say, "Well, who cares if it's malignant if he's ninety-three?" But he thinks of life just as if he were nine, you know. He's still alive. This is a good man, a stake patriarch. It happens that two of the nurses on his floor received their patriarchal blessings from him. He has blessed hundreds and hundreds of people during twenty years as a patriarch. . . .*
>
> *He wakes up from his surgery in terrible pain. He starts muttering. He is*

under sedation and somewhat confused. His first words are, "Thelma, Thelma, Thelma." She is in the room and grabs his hand, but at the age of ninety-two, she can't hold Vic's hand twenty-four hours a day. It's interesting to see what seventy years of marriage can do to the bond. His reflex when he feels pain is to say, "Thelma." If he feels her hand, it's okay.

It still hurts terribly. Just a bit later, I hear him say, "Thelma, what am I going to do? It hurts so much more than I can stand. What am I to do?" She says, "You will have to be patient, dear." I was interested in that because I think that is exactly right. She doesn't say, "Oh, I don't know. It is terrible." That wouldn't help very much. She faces it and wishes it were she, but that is not possible. So she helps him face it: "You will have to be patient, dear."

The doctor comes in and Thelma returns to her chair. Vic grabs the doctor's hand and when he realizes it isn't Thelma's, he is a little upset. He pleads in a whisper, "Thelma, quickly." She starts shuffling over at a ninety-two-year-old pace and says, "Just a minute, Vic." He says, "Thelma, I can't wait just a minute." She has little tears in her eyes. This is a picture of two people who have become one, needing each other, the one helping the other to be patient—just what the Lord wanted, I believe.

Sharon's marriage ended after twenty years of vicious abuse. Then she learned that her children, all that time, were also abused. The man who created this nightmare subsequently abandoned his family financially. Sharon's wounds deepened when some would not believe her story. The healing process came in small miracles over the years.

She can finally say: "It has been so slow, so very slow. But I have learned how to look to the Lord. He strengthened me just enough when there was nowhere to turn. I got my security from him. Here and there, I received a testimony of my worth. Just think of it, even after all that maltreatment over the years."

Sharon's poise and radiance are now legendary among those who know her, revealing the watchful eye and healing influence of a personal God. She reminds us of the comforting of Helaman's army when it was outnumbered, starving, and abandoned by headquarters.

> *We did pour out our souls in prayer to God, that he would strengthen us and deliver us. . . . And it came to pass that the Lord our God did visit us with assurances that he would deliver us; yea, insomuch that he did speak peace to our souls, and did grant unto us great faith, and did cause us that we should hope for our deliverance in him.*[3]

From Nancy, wife of a burn victim:

> *I have often wondered how we made it through those days, weeks, and months while Rob was in the hospital. Even after he came home, life was very difficult. What comes to my mind is that even at the worst times, I always*

came back to the basics of the gospel, taught to me as a small child by my parents and teachers. When trials come into our lives, that's when all these basic teachings really matter to us.

I cannot completely explain the heartache of watching the suffering that Rob went through in the burn unit. Sometimes I felt guilt as I begged the Lord to heal him. I would ask him constantly in prayer to let Rob live and stay with me and our three children. Then I would walk over to the hospital and spend my visiting time watching him suffer. I knew if Rob was taken, all would be well with him, and yet I begged and then watched him suffer more.

There is power in prayer! We often took turns pouring out our hearts to Heavenly Father. Peace and comfort would come, anger would leave, calmness would come over the hospital room, and the words would come as we opened our hearts to our Father. I found it important to remind Rob that he still had the power of the priesthood. That's important for the caregiver to remember: help the sufferer feel his worth. So much dignity is lost in these situations. . . .

I repeatedly found that added strength is given to the caregiver. One experience occurred about three months after Rob was burned. I was walking over to the hospital and it was very hot and humid. I was having a hard time breathing because the air was so thick and I was also very lonely. . . . I could only see Rob twice a day—two-hour periods at lunch and dinnertime. As I was walking, I felt I couldn't go on anymore. I had no physical or emotional strength left. I bowed my head and prayed. I told Heavenly Father that I couldn't do this anymore and pleaded for help. Even before I finished my prayer, I felt someone walking to the left of me, and I could physically feel their touch on my shoulder and down my left arm. I couldn't see anyone but was comforted and guided right to the front doors of the hospital. I know God hears our plea for help and never leaves us without comfort and strength.

One of the hardest things to deal with when a loved one is suffering is the confused anger the sufferer directs at the caregiver. I started to take it personally. I learned to rely on help from doctors and nurses. I asked questions, even if they sounded stupid. It helped me so much to be informed about what was going on at all times and how to deal with it. Rob was so incoherent, and I didn't really know what to say to him. I was told to keep talking to him about reality, reminding him of the day, date, time of day, and so on. I learned that knowledge helps take away fear.

One of the social workers helped me to understand what I had to do to strengthen myself so that I was able to help Rob more. The worker said that many women are like cookie jars. Everyone (husbands, children, community, church people) are always lifting the lid and taking cookies out. Sometimes it's just one at a time, but when we have huge stresses like Rob's injuries, the cookies are depleted by the handfuls. To be able to give cookies, I needed to do things for myself to replenish the cookie jar.

I learned to relax more. I read books, shopped, and went with family members of other burn patients to see the sights. Sometimes I would feel guilty but realized that it was important to "bake cookies." The fun was to be able to go back to Rob's room and tell him about all the things I had seen and done. He especially enjoyed hearing about life going on in the outside world. I bought postcards to show him pictures of things I had seen. I also kept myself cleaned up and attractive. It really helped my attitude, and it was good for Rob to see too.

I have learned that sometimes it's okay to cry and ask the probing questions. Our loving Savior explained his agony to his Father in the Garden of Gethsemane. I am sure there were tears of sorrow and fear. But when we're willing to lay everything out to our Father, he will bless us in ways we could never imagine.

The day I was to start chemotherapy after being diagnosed with breast cancer in 1997, Rob and I sat on the banks of the Snake River right across from the Idaho Falls Temple. I had just had my radiation treatment for the day and had become very emotional. As we talked about the fears I was having, we remembered the Savior's suffering. Even Christ had an angel come down and administer to him.

Turning to the scriptures gave me so much peace. The people in the Book of Mormon became my friends, and I remember being sad as I finished the book because I would really miss them! I remember reading in Mosiah 24, where Amulon is persecuting Alma and his people. The Lord told them to "lift up [their] heads and be of good comfort." He made their burdens light, and he said, "I, the Lord God, do visit my people in their afflictions."⁴

I knew the Lord had done this in my life. Sometimes, like the people in Mosiah 24:15, I really did not feel the burden: "And they did submit cheerfully and with patience to all the will of the Lord." That little word "all" stuck out! We can be cheerful through all of it by asking for his help. He answers those prayers.

From Candice, thinking back on her care after surgery:

One thing we shouldn't do is treat the sick as if their illness somehow has made them stupid. I found that many medical people and even a few visitors treated me as if being in a bed and gown meant I didn't have a brain. They had a way of forgetting my human dignity. They sometimes talked down to me, reminding me of the way some of the orderlies treated my grandfather when he was old and bedridden for so long. I found that the kinder environments (I was in more than one ward of more than one hospital during my illness) seemed to foster more hope and even health.

I was amazed at how sensitive people can be. There was the frazzled, busy nurse who once just decided to put me in a wheelchair and take me outside for fresh air and a long chat. That was very impressive because the busyness didn't blind her to priorities.

The most spiritual floor of the hospital was the cancer ward. There, I grew in my vision of others who suffer. When they put me on the cancer floor, they brought my little girl in to visit me, and the patients there lighted up to see a new precious life. They actually came out of their rooms and followed us around the hall, just to see a bright, fresh life. People came, died, and were replaced with others soon to die. What a somber place.

My illness somehow gave me an understanding of heaven, of how heavenly people care for us in this world, and of how sensitive and caring they are in doing so.

All this may have been harder on my husband than on me. He carried the usual burdens — boring and lonely chores for both of us. So we should also consider the needs of helpless watchers, loved ones who are often forgotten.

Hans and Inger sold all their belonging in their thirties so that Hans could return to school. After the struggles of caring for a large family through that ordeal, Hans graduated from law school and was offered a job with a large firm. The offer meant moving to a distant and unfamiliar nation, but he and Inger decided to accept. They moved their family and found a modest home.

The days were long and stressful for Hans, and long and lonely for Inger and the children. They survived the passing months mostly by courage and blessings. Then the bottom fell out. The company downsized, and Hans lost his job without warning. Displaced and unemployed in an unfriendly part of the world, Hans was confused, depressed, and restless. Then, after a few days, came this glimpse of grace:

> *I woke up before everyone else the other morning and felt inspired to pray. As I prayed, I felt I saw the Lord smile at me and felt such an outpouring of love. I had a great feeling that it doesn't matter what happens to us in this life. This life is so short compared to eternity anyway. It's like you're a child, and someone is giving you a shot. You feel uncomfortable and that life is terrible, but it only lasts a few minutes. Compared to eternity, our pain doesn't last even a split second. So I felt that if we do what's right, we'll be fine in eternity. We'll be happy. And I just felt great.*
>
> *I felt like my body was tense when I started praying, and when I was done it was all relaxed and happy. I felt like praying and praying and praying. It was like I had remembered something precious that I had forgotten. Tears were coming to my eyes. Life was hard for me even without losing a job, but it would be okay. Half of my life is gone. Probably a half more of this time and I will join the Lord. And this half went fast. It had bruises and pains; it had bad moments. But pretty soon, we won't even notice them. We'll join the Lord, and all our pains and sufferings we have experienced will be like a cut finger or a*

bruise when we were five years old. We'll probably remember them, but they'll be insignificant.

I felt it's okay. It doesn't matter. We can lose the house and all that we have. It will still be okay, as long as we have each other and our love. It felt so good to feel his love and his care. I felt like somebody up there was smiling at me saying, "Cheer up! You're okay!" Yes, life is hard, but it is so short. Life really is so much easier when you have that strong perspective.

Notes

1. Moses 7:28.
2. Names have been changed.
3. Alma 58:10–11.
4. Mosiah 24:13–14.

"GOD SHALL EXALT THEE"

What comes after the brief gift of growth?

If thou endure it well, God shall exalt thee on high (D&C 121:8).

Only after the mortal opportunity is past, after we have offered our lifelong response, will grief's grand purpose become obvious to us. Then we will see what a perfect gift it was after all.

31

Avoid the Greater Suffering

Pain, fatigue, confusion, and loneliness are fleeting. But the acid of guilt is another matter. In this life, we taste it in small, measured doses only. Carried into the next life, guilt clings to the stained spirit, eats at the haunted mind, and pierces the unsettled heart with compound force.[1] Joseph Fielding Smith called guilt "a punishment of cleansing."[2] It is inflicted by the iron demands of justice. Scripture associates it with eternal torment, horror, bitterness,[3] fire and brimstone,[4] spiritual death,[5] and hell.[6] It is the greater suffering.

The pain which we suffer in the flesh dwindles into insignificance in comparison with the sufferings which we undergo from a tender conscience that has been seared.[7]

Alma the Younger tasted the fiery terror of hell. A few days of bitter remorse toppled his towering pride. He turned to the Redeemer, who cut short his greater suffering.[8] Alma continued to face mortal hardship, but that passed soon enough. His life is now a lesson in the greater and lesser kinds of suffering.

The sufferings entailed by the fate of condemnation are more to be feared than are any possible inflictions of physical torture; the mind, the spirit, the whole soul is doomed to suffer, and the torment is known by none in the flesh.[9]

Paul escaped the greater suffering, though he submitted to many lesser sufferings.[10]

In prisons more frequent, in deaths oft. . . . Five times received I forty stripes save one. Thrice was I beaten with rods, once was I stoned, thrice I suffered shipwreck, a night and a day I have been in the deep; in journeyings often, in perils of waters, in perils of robbers, in perils by mine own countrymen, in perils by the heathen, in perils in the city, in perils in the wilderness, in perils in the sea, in perils among false brethren; in weariness and painfulness, in watchings often, in hunger and thirst, in fastings often, in cold and nakedness. Beside those things that are without, that which cometh upon me daily, the care of all the churches.[11]

That was nearly two thousand years ago. Paul will never again have mortal pain or peril. And better yet, he avoided the greater suffering.

There is . . . one kind of pain . . . Jesus would help us to avoid: suffering for our sins.[12]

Christ can absorb the acid of clinging guilt,[13] and we can leave mortality clean and safe in the arms of mercy. If the lesser suffering in this life refines us, we need not be slowly purged by the greater suffering in the next.[14] The

Refiner offers his atonement to us if we offer ourselves to him, which may mean passing faithfully through the lesser suffering.[15] He is willing to manage our smaller burdens and to remove the worst burden of all.[16]

Notes

1. Mosiah 2:38.
2. Joseph Fielding Smith, *The Way to Perfection*, 304.
3. Alma 36:12, 18, 24.
4. Mosiah 3:27.
5. Alma 42:9.
6. 3 Nephi 12:30.
7. Abraham H. Cannon, in Stuy, *Collected Discourses*, 4:209.
8. Alma 36:15–19.
9. James E. Talmage, *Articles of Faith*, 59.
10. Acts 9:15–16.
11. 2 Corinthians 11:23–28.
12. Neal A. Maxwell, *Even As I Am*, 103.
13. Matthew 11:28; Enos 1:6–8; D&C 19:16, 20.
14. Alma 34:16, 34.
15. Mosiah 3:19.
16. Alma 7:11–13.

32

Stronger and Stronger

Though we may exit the body in distress, how glad will be our discovery of a renewed spirit, more forceful and glorious than ever. This great change in the spirit is possible because of our special dual nature.

The spirit must rise to its full height in order to subdue our physical side. If we cannot satisfy both physical and spiritual aims, which do we want the most? The suffering person must make choices every hour. Complain or praise? Become absorbed in self or grow in tune with God? Those choices mold the soul, even in a declining body.

Moral and spiritual strength can grow stronger as the physical part of us weakens with age.[1]

A strong spirit is far superior to a tough body or a powerful intellect.[2] It is your spirit—the real you—that suffers when your body ails and that chooses patience.[3] Your spirit is the part that grows strong through that choice. A strong, peaceful spirit is ready and steady in the storms. The wonder of mortality is that regardless of what betides God's faithful children, they simply *grow*—sometimes by tiny stitches and sometimes by surges but always from strength to strength.

The righteous also shall hold on his way, and he that hath clean hands shall be stronger and stronger.[4]

In gyms all over the world, coaches teach proven principles for increasing strength. The key principle is that strength increases against resistance—heavy resistance develops power, repeated resistance develops endurance. "No pain, no gain." This is also the way of spirit muscle. Our strength comes from the way we pass through our trials.

He maketh sore, . . . and his hands make whole.[5]

Doctrine and Covenants 113 speaks of a servant of Christ, Joseph Smith, "on whom there is laid much power."[6] Firm hands coached Joseph through heavy burdens. Another Joseph, "whose feet they hurt with fetters," acquired strength in an Egyptian prison. Power was laid upon him as "he was laid in iron."[7] Other translations suggest that "into iron came his soul" or "iron or mettle was put into his soul."[8]

Our weak spots—the selfish regions of our souls—have to be worked. Crying is sometimes the solemn sound of growth, the spirit facing resistance. In suffering, we must try to resist petty reflexes. At first we will need to pause and react deliberately. But eventually the reflexes will become automatic. Our

Father will be our strength coach if we let him. He assigns repetitious burdens at times, very heavy ones at other times. He whispers advice and cheers us on against pain. He stands near and steadies, but he does not excuse us from our work. If he did that, we would not grow. The strength-building routines of the gospel are "adapted to the capacity of the weak and the weakest of all."[9]

To them that have no might he increaseth strength.[10]

When the tour of growth is over, we will be able to say, "Well, trouble, my old friend, you have been an interesting roommate. It seems you have brought out the best in me after all. I thank you for that, and now I bid you a lasting good-bye. I shall not be boarding with you again."

Notes

1. Boyd K. Packer, "Agency and Control," *Ensign*, April 1983, 67.
2. Proverbs 16:32.
3. James 1:2–4.
4. Job 17:9.
5. Job 5:18.
6. D&C 113:4.
7. Psalm 105:18.
8. Jay P. Green, *Interlinear Hebrew*, 3:1489.
9. D&C 89:3.
10. Isaiah 40:29.

33

The Inward Miracle

When our Father permits his higher forces to mingle with our lesser ones, a miracle results—something beyond the reach of normal human effort. The best miracle is the less visible kind that changes the inward, lasting part of us.

> *Though our outward man perish, yet the inward man is renewed day by day. For our light affliction . . . worketh for us a far more exceeding and eternal weight of glory; . . . For the things which are seen are temporal; but the things which are not seen are eternal.[1]*

For example, if I break my leg but then experience instant healing, I suffer no pain, endure no sleepless nights, and have no need of help from others. As a result, I enjoy no growth, which could have come had the Lord used my broken leg to deepen my character and widen my outlook.

> *God having provided some better things for them through their sufferings, for without sufferings they could not be made perfect.[2]*

On occasion, an outward miracle may be just what I need; it may draw me to the God of greater miracles. Knowing he can heal my leg, I may let him heal me! But that is just the point: I am the one who most needs to change and experience real growth in my trust, patience, and courage. So which miracle will be the most frequent, the inward kind or the outward kind? In faithful lives, the slow, sometimes stern marvels of interior change are far more common. Our Father never forgets our need to grow.

> *After their temptations, and much tribulation, behold, I, the Lord, will feel after them, and if they harden not their hearts, and stiffen not their necks against me, they shall be converted, and I will heal them.*[3]

Deep change comes in steps, and steps take time. Inward treasures are gathered slowly, but the God of lasting miracles is in no hurry. What to us seems a sad problem may to him actually be a sanctifying project, deserving his close attention and highest forces. He releases those forces when we yield our hearts to him.

> *Unto the filling their souls with joy and consolation, yea, even to the purifying and the sanctification of their hearts, which sanctification cometh because of their yielding their hearts unto God.*[4]

Since hurry could ruin everything, God waits until the project is finished while we wonder at the slow pace.[5] In a winter dungeon, Joseph Smith pleaded, "How long shall thy hand be stayed?"[6] The Lord may answer with silence, as if to say, "The miracle is not quite complete." The silence in Liberty Jail was finally broken as the Lord met Joseph's question with another question: "How long can rolling waters remain impure?"[7] Perhaps he was saying, "You want to know how long my people must be in turmoil, as waters rolling over rocks and falls? Until they are pure." The outward miracle must wait until the inward is finished.

In premortality we needed a miracle. We needed more wisdom, firmness, patience, power, and grace, which we could not gain there. We are in mortality for that very miracle. We will someday see the vast change that is even now taking place. To be sure, it will need our cooperation. But a wondrous miracle it will be.

> *Then shall ye know . . . that I am the true light that is in you . . . ; otherwise ye could not abound.*[8]

Notes

1. 2 Corinthians 4:16–18.
2. JST, Hebrews 11:40.
3. D&C 112:13.
4. Helaman 3:35.
5. Psalm 13:1–2.
6. D&C 121:2.
7. D&C 121:33.
8. D&C 88:50.

34

Precious Is the Death of His Saints

The righteous who die are pleased with the results of their mortal tour of growth. Death moves them further toward fullness of joy. The gospel, so fearless and positive, unveils death as a splendid ascent.[1] No matter by what means his life may end, "no righteous man is ever taken before his time."[2] We need not rush toward that day nor hide from it. When it comes, the Lord will join us in our gladness.

Precious in the sight of the Lord is the death of his saints.[3]

What awaits the faithful is a spirit *paradise* — literally an enclosed garden or park, suggesting natural splendor, freshness, and peace.[4] Besides being nice to look at, paradise will free us of all our troubles and sorrows![5] Along with beauty and rest, we will find a dramatic upgrade in our powers and joys, which "in the absence of the body are more acute."[6]

We shall turn round and look upon [the valley of death] and think, when we have crossed it, why this is the greatest advantage of my whole existence, for I have passed from a state of sorrow, grief, mourning, woe, misery, pain, anguish and disappointment. . . . My spirit is set free, . . . nothing like pain or weariness, I am full of life, full of vigor, and I enjoy the presence of my heavenly Father.[7]

Just before Jacob's death, he declared, "I am to be gathered unto my people,"[8] the perfect description of death for a covenant person. Two generations later, his grandson Joseph joined him, saying, "I die, and go unto my fathers; and I go down to my grave with joy."[9] In the reunion and jubilation, we will even discover friends and family we did not know on earth who have long cherished us. Crowning all these encounters will be our meeting with him who cherishes us most of all.[10]

Thou shalt live together in love, insomuch that thou shalt weep for the loss of them that die.[11]

The Lord never suggested we could replace the toddler who brightened every hour, the father whose support meant everything temporal and spiritual, the companion with whom we became one. He delights in our affection and even our longing for loved ones. But they do not belong to us alone. He will, in just a little while, restore them to us (or us to them) forever. In the meantime, we are promised comfort, and the deceased are promised crowns. Tears moisten faces that are calm and sure. Our knowledge towers above the shadows of death.

Those that die in me shall not taste of death, for it shall be sweet unto them.[12]

At birth, we descended from glory to a perfectly imperfect life. Death not only restores but may even elevate us higher than we were before. Death is not morbid. To the righteous in particular, it overthrows all that is morbid. It is a bright ascent to comforts and crowns.[13] The gospel gives us the best of both worlds — we live in the embrace of Christ and when we die, we die in his arms.[14]

Notes

1. Alma 27:28; D&C 101:36–37.
2. Joseph Fielding Smith, "Elder Evans Dies, Eulogized at Rites," *Church News*, 6 November 1971, 3.
3. Psalm 116:15.
4. Luke 23:43; Moroni 10:34; Bible Dictionary, s.v. "Paradise."
5. Alma 40:11–12.
6. Brigham Young, *Journal of Discourses*, 1:5.
7. Young, *Journal of Discourses*, 17:142.
8. Genesis 49:29.
9. JST, Genesis 50:24.
10. D&C 88:56, 58, 60, 68.
11. D&C 42:45.
12. D&C 42:46.
13. D&C 101:14–15.
14. D&C 42:44; Mormon 5:11.

35

He Offers His All

Our Father governs all things we know of and all other things lying beyond the reach of our minds and machines. The grandest thing we know about is his offer to share "all that [he] hath" with us.[1] For the person who has everything in this world (or the person who has nothing), exaltation is the perfect gift. All worldly wealth is mere gloss and pretense by comparison.

> *Then shall they be above all, because all things are subject unto them. Then shall they be gods, because they have all power, and the angels are subject unto them.*[2]

The Redeemer will clothe us in celestial bodies like his own.[3] In these exalted bodies will reside a light capable of founding and upholding endless creations.[4] But exaltation is not primarily about creation, matter, and power. The very point of faithfulness is to learn that these are means, not ends. Celestial reward is not unlimited real estate but unrestrained righteousness. It is union with wondrous beings and service to others in magnitudes beyond our present grasp. It is the joy of unselfishness, the bliss of being clean, the fulfillment of family instincts, the "peace of God, which passeth all under-standing."[5]

The riches of eternity are mine to give.[6]

The word *exalted*—to be raised or lifted up—denotes being raised by another, not by oneself.[7] God is the Exalting One. He exalts in love and generosity. Some have concluded that the doctrine of exaltation is irreverent or blasphemous.[8] But what could be more disrespectful toward God than to suppose that he is not generous enough to offer all he has to his children? His generosity exceeds all calculation.[9] In fact, each exalted soul is to become like God![10] Thus, there are no varying degrees of exaltation.

The saints shall be filled with his glory, and receive their inheritance and be made equal with him.[11]

What will we give in exchange for better, nobler, more glorious versions of ourselves? To be true in tribulation is not asking very much.[12] Afterward comes what even God describes as "much glory."[13] The Savior will testify of our integrity before heavenly hosts and introduce us as coheirs with them.[14] We will receive all this for enduring it well for a small moment.[15]

All thrones and dominions, principalities and powers, shall be revealed and set forth upon all who have endured valiantly for the gospel of Jesus Christ.[16]

He does not simply intend for us to have what he has but to be what he is. No one but God can mold someone in his likeness. The energy of his corrections and the object of his solemn shaping and sculpting is a measure of his devotion to our future. He has made it his work to offer us all.

The whole object of the creation of this world is to exalt the intelligences that are placed upon it, that they may live, endure, and increase for ever and ever.[17]

Notes

1. D&C 84:38; 76:58–59; Romans 8:32.
2. D&C 132:20.
3. Philippians 3:21.
4. D&C 76:70; 88:28.
5. Philippians 4:7.
6. D&C 67:2.
7. *Noah Webster's First Edition,* s.v. "Exalted."
8. Philippians 2:5–6.
9. D&C 133:45.
10. Revelation 3:21; D&C 29:12.
11. D&C 88:107.
12. Acts 14:22; James 1:12.
13. D&C 58:4.
14. Revelation 3:5; Romans 8:16–17.
15. D&C 121:7–8.
16. D&C 121:29.
17. Brigham Young, *Journal of Discourses,* 7:290.

36

He Will Wipe Away the Tears

Becoming a parent is no casual matter. Children mature as sons rather than clones and grow up as daughters, not duplicates. The transformation of a child is punctuated by cries. Our Father sees each tear and registers each pain. How odd, in light of the Son's suffering, that we call the Father's attention to our suffering![1]

After the tears come recovery and rest. The severely handicapped man lay year by year upon the same humble little spot by the pool of Bethesda as a representative of the millions who have lain in like conditions.[2] His suffering has long since been made up to him, and it will likewise be made up to all who so suffer.

> *And he will destroy . . . the vail that is spread over all nations. . . . And the Lord God will wipe away tears from off all faces.*[3]

We cannot know the truth about suffering until we know the truth about "things as they are, and as they were, and as they are to come."[4] To know any less is woefully confusing. Therefore, soon after God takes away the veil of mystery over each righteous life, hearts will stop aching, tears will stop flowing, grudges will evaporate, and nagging accounts will be closed.[5] In an instant, we will let go of claims and complaints.

The former shall not be remembered, nor come into mind.[6]

Even abuse and brutality will take their place among the shrinking details of the past. Hard memories and resentment will, like ice, melt before the blaze of our Father's light. Meanwhile, the abuser will find his vain hopes shrinking into terrors, his agency reduced, his ill wishes frustrated, and his guilt spoken from the housetops.[7] Divine irony will intervene with an iron hand; things will turn upside down.[8]

Ye shall be sorrowful, but your sorrow shall be turned into joy.[9]

As the Master stills waves of tears, as celestial surprises overrule tension and gloom, every knee will bow to honor him who sets things right, and every soul will approve of his actions and reactions in every life.[10]

Suppose that you could see yourselves thousands and millions of years after you have proved faithful . . . ; then look back upon your . . . losses, crosses, and disappointments, the sorrows. . . . You would be constrained to exclaim, "But what of all that? Those things were but for a moment, and we are now here."[11]

Even today we can borrow solace from that future day. Why not bow the knee in praise now? Why not, by faith, cry a little less and see a little more — more clearly and more early — through the veil of tears?[12]

Notes

1. Mosiah 3:7; Alma 7:12; D&C 18:11.

2. John 5:2–9.

3. Isaiah 25:7–8.

4. D&C 93:24; Jacob 4:13.

5. Revelation 7:17; 21:4.

6. Isaiah 65:17.

7. D&C 1:3.

8. D&C 45:50; 121:10–14; Psalm 126:5–6; 1 Samuel 2:8.

9. John 16:20.

10. 1 Nephi 1:14–15; Mosiah 27:31; Revelation 5:13.

11. Brigham Young, *Journal of Discourses*, 7:275.

12. 2 Corinthians 4:8.

37

Linked to Him

Surrounded by violent waves, the terrified disciples asked, "Carest thou not that we perish?"[1] Perhaps we have asked the same thing, but it is for us, not Jesus, to answer. Does he care? Can we trust his friendship?[2] Our answer tells how well we know him. Without storms, we have difficulty becoming acquainted with Deity.

In all their afflictions he was afflicted. . . . In his love, and in his pity, he redeemed them, and bore them, and carried them all the days of old.[3]

The truth is that he delights in you and me.[4] He prepares a way and a place for joining him, and he waits for us to prepare ourselves.[5] He is closer than we think.[6] Perhaps we have our comfort and pleasure alone, but our pain—nerve by nerve—is shared with a faithful friend.[7] Yet, he is never hardened by his awareness of sorrow. Our suffering may not be as real to us as it is to him!

By the rod of trouble, we can bond with him and know that he is our friend. As proxy for us, he bore our heavy cross and asks us to take up light ones. As his proxies, we sometimes do the uncomfortable things he would do if he were here. He empathizes with us in a sacred and quiet fellowship.

> *We are individually in His presence. . . . Thank God for that principle. . . . For such a principle to be omitted from the work of the Lord would be an omission too serious to contemplate. It could not be.*[8]

Suffering makes our quiet companion more discernible. The veil, especially the part covering the heart, is thinner. He leans near with encouragement, suggestions, leadership, strength, and peace. He consoles, "Be of good cheer,"[9] and he whispers, "I will lead you along."[10] If we, like Paul, ask a thorn to be removed, he may quietly suggest another approach: "My grace is sufficient for thee: for my strength is made perfect in weakness."[11] If we hunger and thirst after righteousness, he fills us with the Holy Ghost.[12] If the path is steep with grief and suffering, he leaves the peak to join us and say, "Ye shall obtain."[13] Thus does he gently make himself known.

> *Who can say too much of his great power, and of his mercy, and of his long-suffering towards the children of men? . . . I cannot say the smallest part which I feel. . . . We have been patient in our sufferings, and we have suffered every privation. . . . Blessed be the name of my God, who has been mindful of us. . . . I will give thanks unto my God forever. Amen.*[14]

By our adventures with him in the storms, we discover that he cares, and we find ourselves wanting to honor him forever. In every ordeal we see his hand steadying us and our oppressive burdens. We testify, "My God hath been my support."[15] Our affection for him swallows up affliction.[16] All our losses are gains if they link us to him.[17]

Notes

1. Mark 4:38.
2. Jeremiah 17:7–8.
3. D&C 133:53.
4. Psalm 17:8.
5. John 14:2–3; D&C 67:13.
6. Joshua 1:9; Psalm 34:15, 19.
7. Isaiah 53:4–7; Luke 24:45–48.
8. Joseph F. Smith, in *Messages of the First Presidency*, 5:86–87.
9. John 16:33.
10. D&C 78:18.
11. 2 Corinthians 12:9.
12. 3 Nephi 12:6.
13. *Hymns*, no. 134.
14. Alma 26:16, 28, 36–37.
15. 2 Nephi 4:20; 2 Samuel 22:2–4; 1 Nephi 1:20.
16. Alma 26:16, 28, 36–37; 31:38; 37:36.
17. Philippians 1:21; 3:7.

38

The Faithful Crossing

C rossing from the premortal life to the postmortal life is a once-only ordeal in eternity. Rather than hop across a trench, we go into a low canyon and climb steep slopes.

Instead of this,   it is more like this.

The old word for "to cross" is *'Eber.* It may have given rise to Abraham's title, "the Hebrew."[1] As children of Abraham and Sarah, we continue his tradition of crossing barriers of various kinds. In the second estate, we face cultural barriers and pain barriers as well as trials, veils, and valleys. A faithful crossing is no small matter.

The word of God . . . shall . . . lead the man of Christ in a strait and narrow course across that everlasting gulf of misery which is prepared to engulf the wicked.[2]

The God of Abraham is our God also. He is right up the trail, just on the other side of the horizon, hoping we will reach for his hand as Abraham did. If we endure the trail well, we will experience a miracle of growth made possible by the Redeemer. Over and over again, he adds the inner miracle. It takes a team effort with the God of the Hebrews, the God of those who make crossings.[3] Each rise of the path to exaltation, if we look closely, appears something like this:

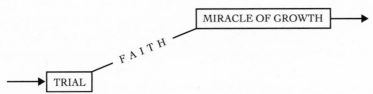

Abraham's grandson, Jacob, came to the ford called Jabbok. On the other side lay all the blessings of eternity. What a crossing! In one night, he gave his whole heart and substance. At sunrise, he was the hero called Israel.[4]

Israel means "one who prevails with God" or "let God prevail."[5] Certainly, we cannot prevail without God. He watches, plans, and works as he urges us to cross.

I can do all things through Christ which strengtheneth me.[6]

Notes

1. Genesis 14:13; Bible Dictionary, s.v. "Hebrew"; *Noah Webster's First Edition,* s.v. "Hebrew."
2. Helaman 3:29.
3. D&C 76:50–60; 136:1–2, 20–22.
4. Genesis 32:22–31.
5. Bible Dictionary, s.v. "Israel."
6. Philippians 4:13.

39

A Perfect Schoolhouse

Mortal life is a marvel of elegance, but by heavenly standards it is coarse and unruly. James E. Talmage called the mortal body a "student's garb of flesh."[1] Wisely designed imperfections—mental, emotional, and physical— make our bodies the perfect schoolhouse. They indicate to heavenly friends that we are still in school, facing problems not found in heaven.

It is good for me that I have been afflicted; that I might learn thy statutes.[2]

Mental imperfections severely limit memory and thought for the spirit within. When Nehor offered his falsehoods to the Nephites, "many did believe on his words, even so many that they began to support him and give him money."[3] In their first estate, none of these people (not even Nehor) would have bought such nonsense. But in the mental limits of the second estate, they embraced what they once rejected. In this schoolhouse, we pass tests by trusting truth rather than brains.

Emotional imperfections permit salty tides to toss the spirit to and fro. But we still have a choice: swim or drift. Our best efforts in the strong waves of emotion may seem weak. But what matters is our exertion, not our position, in the ocean of emotion. Will we at least try to imitate the calm and dignity of our Exemplar and turn to him for stability? Strong undercurrents surge from our upbringing, genetic influence, and chemical activity in the central nervous system. These are not always in our control, but in some degree we can react according to the light we have. To that degree, we choose whether to passively float along or actively battle the negative current.

Physical imperfections present all sorts of distractions relating to pleasure, pain, and fatigue. But we are dual beings.[4] The finer part of us must get control of the coarser part before the two fuse together in resurrection. The daily question is, "Shall I do with my physical temple what God would ask?"

This earthly school offers us our finest hours, even on ordinary days. The lab of the bitter cup teaches us to discern good from evil, polish from stain, living water from poison. Our hearts develop perfect hearing and bearing. Graduation with highest honors awaits every learner who wears the garb of flesh with patience and faith.

In much wisdom is much grief.[5]

The Lord gave Joseph Smith a sample list of troubles that might be permitted in the life of a righteous person, such as being hunted by bloodthirsty men, opposed by the forces of nature, or jailed unjustly.[6] Then the Lord explained that trouble serves two purposes.

All these things shall give thee experience, and shall be for thy good.[7]

Trouble teaches. What did Joseph learn from his troubles? Above all, he learned that "the God of my fathers delivered me out of them all, and will deliver me from henceforth."[8] Serious trouble can give us serious experience with God. The more experience we have, the more we may witness his deliverance.[9] Experience reveals the living God to be a faithful God.

But trials will only give us the knowledge necessary to understand the minds of the ancients. For my part, I think I never could have felt as I now do, if I had not suffered the wrongs that I have suffered.[10]

Trouble transforms. We are here to do more than *experience* the goodness of God. We must *acquire* it.

It seems to me my heart will always be more tender after this than ever it was before.[11]

Because of the matchless way it teaches and transforms, a mortal life rich with difficulty is the best educational bargain in eternity. It fits us to be witnesses, heirs, and friends of God. That is why it is worth the trouble.

Notes

1. Conference Report, October 1932, 78.
2. Psalm 119:71.

3. Alma 1:5.

4. D&C 93:33–35.

5. Ecclesiastes 1:18.

6. D&C 122:5–7.

7. D&C 122:7.

8. D&C 127:2.

9. 2 Timothy 3:11; D&C 68:6.

10. Joseph Smith, *History of the Church,* 3:286.

11. Smith, *History of the Church,* 3:286.

40

Glimpses of Glory

John saw the celestial throng emerge "out of great tribulation."[1] Of course, most of us are unnoticed during our mortal struggles, for fame would spoil the polishing. But tribulation returns us to God, shining and perfect.

> *This royal path has long been trod*
> *By righteous men, each now a God:*
> *As Abra'm, Isaac, Jacob, too,*
> *First babes, then men — to gods they grew.*
> *As man now is, our God once was;*
> *As now God is, so man may be, —*
> *Which doth unfold man's destiny.*[2]

We can hardly give firsthand accounts of people around us entering into their glory, but we do have scriptural accounts — the ultimate success stories — of glorified beings who once lived in this world. We know of the celestial success of Abraham, Isaac, and Jacob, along with their equally glorious companions, Sarah, Rebecca, and Rachel. We have descriptions of Adam, John the Baptist, Moroni, and others. We have a worshipful account of the blazing throne of God and the glorified Christ, who make all celestial success possible. We are left to wonder what it will mean to be among these beings in a time to come and to partake of that success ourselves.

The heavens were opened upon us, and I beheld the celestial kingdom of God, and the glory thereof. . . . I saw the transcendent beauty of the gate through which the heirs of that kingdom will enter, which was like unto circling flames of fire; also the blazing throne of God, whereon was seated the Father and the Son.[3]

The prophet Daniel foresaw the priesthood gathering to be held at Adam-ondi-Ahman and tried to describe the one presiding:

The Ancient of days did sit, whose garment was white as snow, and the hair of his head like the pure wool: his throne was like the fiery flame. . . . A fiery stream issued and came forth from before him.[4]

So great is the splendor of this being that some readers of the Bible have assumed that he must be the Father or the Son. Indeed, the exalted glory we read of here is like that of God.[5] But the Ancient of Days is the exalted Adam.[6] Eve is no less glorious. For example, the words "they" and "them" refer to husband and wife:

Then shall they be gods, because they have no end; therefore shall they be from everlasting to everlasting, because they continue; then shall they be above all, because all things are subject unto them. Then shall they be gods, because they have all power, and the angels are subject unto them.[7]

Is this celestial couple, now glistening with brightness above the sun and issuing streams of fire and influence, that same Adam and Eve who once left their secure Eden to find new quarters on the unfamiliar hills and fields of a fallen place? Is this radiant woman that Eve who was first among mortal women to know the frightening pains of childbirth? Is this the same couple that toiled simply to survive in a thorny world, and that so often made sacrifices without quite knowing why? Surely their joys are mingled with heartwrenching memories, such as losing one son at the murderous hands of another or having their testimony rejected by some of their posterity.[8] We can only imagine the nine hundred seasons of planting and harvest, the homesteading and travel, the trials and triumphs.

But because Adam and Eve passed through all this in faith, patience, and cheer, their circumstances are now beyond all description. Their tears are wiped away. How their hearts must sing with gratitude for the great plan of redemption and for the great Redeemer.

Will Nancy, once hovering in care over her writhing and delirious husband, leave those tear-stained moments to the past? Will she and Rob someday enjoy the fellowship of celestial beings and the same conditions that Adam and Eve enjoy? Why not, if they are true and faithful? Is not the great day of heavenly employment available to Hans, who was once stunned by unemployment and uncertainty? Or will not the day of reconciliation wipe away all tears from the face of Marissa, who was once bereft of her precious infant son? If they and we are patient with our present lot, we all may be as Adam and Eve have become.

John the Baptist was raised on the sparse products of the shimmering-hot Judean desert. He labored at some trade until age thirty, when he began his difficult work of preparing an unreceptive people for their Messiah. His life was suddenly interrupted by disgraceful arrest and degrading imprisonment. Without worldly honor, he was summarily beheaded.

Oliver Cowdery, who saw the resurrected John the Baptist face to face in 1829, gave us this glimpse of glory:

> On a sudden, as from the midst of eternity . . . the angel of God came down clothed with glory. . . . While all men were resting upon uncertainty, . . . our eyes beheld, our ears heard, . . . above the glitter of the May sunbeam. . . . Then his voice, though mild, pierced to the center, and his words, "I am thy fellow-servant," dispelled every fear. We listened, we gazed, we admired!
>
> . . . I shall not attempt to paint to you . . . the majestic beauty and glory which surrounded us on this occasion; . . . earth, nor men, with the eloquence of time, cannot begin to clothe language in as interesting and sublime a manner as this holy personage. No; nor has this earth power to give the joy, to

*bestow the peace, or comprehend the wisdom which was contained in each sen-
tence as they were delivered by the power of the Holy Spirit!*[9]

As we glimpse the glory of our fellow servant John, we glimpse our own
glory, provided we follow the same path of integrity that he followed. Can the
once-languishing pancreatitis patient, Karrie, also be such a being in time to
come? What of Vic, who once groped for the comfort of Thelma's hand? What
about gloom-shrouded Tammy or cancer-stricken Dave? Not so long from now,
we may all be coheirs with John, not only having celestial peace but radiating it
to others.

To what purpose did Jesus descend so far below our worst sufferings?
After descending, he ascended above the entire array of human experience in
order to fill "all things," including us, with his glorious influence.[10] We might
say that he suffered so that our suffering would make sense.

*And then shall the angels be crowned with the glory of his might, and the saints
shall be filled with his glory, and receive their inheritance and be made equal
with him.*[11]

After being way down here, he is way up there—awaiting, beckoning,
succoring. He invites Elena and Ann and Sharon, along with all other abused
or afflicted souls, to join him. Indeed, "a great multitude, which no man could
number," of every background and plight, will join him in purity and security.[12]

Meanwhile, if we cannot quite glimpse the coming glory, there is something we can do. We can, in this lower place, honor him with our trust for this small mortal moment.

All things wherewith you have been afflicted shall work together for your good, and to my name's glory, saith the Lord.[13]

Notes

1. Revelation 7:14.
2. Lorenzo Snow, *Improvement Era*, June 1919, 660; Bruce R. McConkie, *Doctrinal New Testament Commentary*, 2:532.
3. D&C 137:1–3.
4. Daniel 7:9–10.
5. Daniel 7:13.
6. D&C 116:1; 138:38.
7. D&C 132:20.
8. Moses 5:12–13.
9. Excerpt from footnote to Joseph Smith–History 1:71.
10. Ephesians 1:9–10; D&C 88:6, 29.
11. D&C 88:107.
12. Revelation 7:9.
13. D&C 98:3.

Sources

Clark, James R., comp. *Messages of the First Presidency of The Church of Jesus Christ of Latter-day Saints.* 6 vols. Salt Lake City: Bookcraft, 1965–75.

Conference Reports of The Church of Jesus Christ of Latter-day Saints. Salt Lake City: The Church of Jesus Christ of Latter-day Saints, 1898–.

Dew, Sheri L. *Go Forward with Faith.* Salt Lake City: Deseret Book, 1996.

Ensign. Salt Lake City: The Church of Jesus Christ of Latter-day Saints, 1971–.

Green, J. P., Sr., ed. and trans. *The Interlinear Hebrew-Greek-English Bible.* 4 vols. Peabody, Mass.: Hendrickson Publishers, 1985.

Gesenius, H. W. F. *Gesenius' Hebrew and Chaldee Lexicon to the Old Testament Scriptures.* Grand Rapids, Mich.: Baker Book House, 1979.

Hymns of The Church of Jesus Christ of Latter-day Saints. Salt Lake City: The Church of Jesus Christ of Latter-day Saints, 1985.

Improvement Era. Salt Lake City: The Church of Jesus Christ of Latter-day Saints, 1897–1970.

Journal of Discourses. 26 vols. London: Latter-day Saints' Book Depot, 1854–86.

Kimball, Spencer W. *The Teachings of Spencer W. Kimball.* Salt Lake City: Bookcraft, 1982.

Lewis, C. S. *The Problem of Pain.* New York: Macmillan, 1962.

Maxwell, Neal A. *All These Things Shall Give Thee Experience.* Salt Lake City: Bookcraft, 1980.

——. *Even As I Am.* Salt Lake City: Deseret Book, 1982.

McConkie, Bruce R. *Doctrinal New Testament Commentary.* 3 vols. Salt Lake City: Bookcraft, 1965–73.

——. *The Mortal Messiah.* 4 vols. Salt Lake City: Deseret Book, 1979–81.

Noah Webster's First Edition of an American Dictionary of the English Language (1828). Republished in facsimile. San Francisco: Foundation for American Christian Education, 1967.

Smith, Joseph. *History of the Church of Jesus Christ of Latter-day Saints.* Edited by B. H. Roberts. 7 vols. 2d ed. rev. Salt Lake City: The Church of Jesus Christ of Latter-day Saints, 1932–51.

——. *Lectures on Faith.* Salt Lake City: Deseret Book, 1985.

——. *Teachings of the Prophet Joseph Smith.* Selected by Joseph Fielding Smith. Salt Lake City: Deseret Book, 1976.

Smith, Joseph Fielding. *The Way to Perfection.* Salt Lake City: Deseret Book, 1975.

——. *Doctrines of Salvation.* Compiled by Bruce R. McConkie. 3 vols. Salt Lake City: Bookcraft, 1954–56.

Strong, James. *A Concise Dictionary of the Words in the Hebrew Bible,* in *The Exhaustive Concordance of the Bible.* Nashville: Abingdon Press, 1980.

Stuy, Brian H., comp. and ed. *Collected Discourses: Delivered by President Wilford Woodruff, His Two Counselors, the Twelve Apostles, and Others.* 5 vols. Salt Lake City: B.H.S. Publishing, 1987–1992.

Talmage, James E. *The Articles of Faith.* 12th ed. Salt Lake City: The Church of Jesus Christ of Latter-day Saints, 1982.

Woodruff, Wilford. *Wilford Woodruff's Journal, 1833-1898.* Edited by Scott G. Kenney. 9 vols. Midvale, Utah: Signature Books, 1984.

Index

Abraham, 10, 140, 141, 147
Abuse, 31–32, 66–67, 107–8, 135
Adam, 147, 148
Adam and Eve, 9, 20, 149, 150
Adam-ondi-Ahman, 148
Adopted child, story of, 32–33
Adversity, 60–62
Agency, 17–18, 90, 122, 135, 143
Alma, 112, 119
Ammon, 95
Amulon, 112
Ancient of Days, 148
Angels, 92–94, 131
Anger, 34, 110
Ann, story of, 66–67, 151
Anxiety, 55
Atonement, 17–18, 20, 67, 73

Babylon, 27
Back surgery sufferer, story of, 69–70
Beauty, 56
Bethesda, 134
Blame, 101
Body, physical, 14, 143
Book of Mormon, 67, 72–73, 86, 111–12
Book of remembrance, 61

Burn victim, story of, 33–35, 108–12

Calm, 51–53
Cancer, 69–70, 102–3, 106–7, 151
Candice, story of, 112–13
Celestial kingdom, 131, 147–48
Change, 126
Chastisement, 83–85
Cheer, 54–56
Child abuse, 31–32, 66–67, 107
Children, 134
Choices, 17–18, 122, 143
Chronic fatigue syndrome, 71
Comfort, 95–97
Contention, 22
Cowdery, Oliver, on glory, 150–51
Crying, 134–36

Daniel, 148
Dave, story of, 69–70, 151
Death, 20–21, 128–30
Deliverance, 86–88
Depression, 70–73, 95
Despair, 49, 54
Discipleship, 57
Divorce, 107–8

Doubt, 51–53
Dwarfism, story of, 67–69

Eden, 9
Elena, story of, 31–32, 151
Emily, story of, 35
Endurance, 37, 46–47, 117
Evil, 22–23
Exaltation, 117, 131, 132
Experience, 145

Faith, 48–50, 49, 51–53, 144
Fall of man, 20, 48
Father in Heaven. *See* God the Father
Fatigue, 71
Faultfinding, 101
Fear, 63–65, 64, 87, 89, 93
First estate. *See* Premortal life
Foundations, 13–14
Friendship: price of, 25, 98–100; with God, 57; of Job, 98–99, 101–5; of Jesus Christ, 137

Gethsemane, 46, 111
Gloom, 54, 135
Glory, 147–52
God the Father: and suffering, 1; becoming like, 7; confidence of, 49; patience of, 52; friendship of, 57; watchful eyes of, 75; comprehends all, 81; and the Son, 94; governs all, 131
Gold, 39–40, 84
Golf analogy, 19
Good cheer, 54–56

Grace, 106–16, 138
Growth, 5, 31–36, 122–24
Guilt, 101, 119–21, 135

Hans and Inger, story of, 113–15, 150
Happiness, 9, *77*
Haste, 60, 61
Health, 60
Heart, 42–44
Helaman's army, 108
Hesitation, 104
Hinckley, Gordon B., on fear, 87
Holy Ghost, 94
Honor, 60
Hope, 52, 54, 55, 60, 63
Humility, 101–2

Idaho Falls Temple, 111
Innocent, trials of the, 24–25
Integrity, 66–73
Irony, 90, 91, 135
Isaac, 147
Israel, meaning of, 141

Jabbok, 141
Jacob (Bible patriarch), 129, 141, 147
Jacob (son of Lehi), 32
Jeshua, meaning of, 87
Jesus Christ: keeps us from failing, 8; sacrifice of, 11; atonement of, 17–18, 20, 67, 73; grew in stages, 46; suffering of, 66; and the Father, 94; was Job's friend, 104; we die in arms of, 130; linked to, 137–39

Job (Bible character): innocence of, 24; God
    searched heart of, 42; faith of, 49; prepared
    himself, 65; plan for, 89; was protected, 92;
    friends of, 98–99, 101–5
Job loss, story of, 113–15
John the Baptist, 147, 150–51
John the Revelator, 147
Joseph of Egypt, 123, 129
Joshua, meaning of, 87
Joy, *77–79*
Justice, 119

Karrie, story of, 35–36, 151
Kindness, 103

Laman and Lemuel, 32
Last days, 27–28
Law, 16–18
Lee, story of, 67–69
Lehi, 32
Leukemia, 102–3
Lewis, C.S., on God's love, 89
Liberty Jail, 126–27
Loins, 63–64
Loneliness, 99
Long-suffering, 51
Love, 64, 83
Loyalty, 57, 58, 66

Marissa, story of, 32–33, 150
Martha, 64
Memories, 135
Miracles, 125–27

Money, 60, 100, 131
Moroni, 147
Mortal life, 7, 14, 29, 39–40, 58, 66, 90, 140–41,
    143–46
Music, 56

Nancy, story of, 108–12, 149–50
Nehor, 143
Nephi, 13, 57, 86, 96
Nephites, 143

Offerings, 131–33
Opposition, 17, 54

Pains, 80–82, 125
Pancreatitis, 35–26, 151
Paradise, 128
Parents, 134
Past, 135
Patience, 51, 52, 53, 70, 107, 122, 138, 144
Patriarchal blessings, 106
Paul, 57–58, 120, 138
Peter, 60
Pioneers, 58
Plan A, 89–91
Plan of salvation, 13, 42, 78
Possessions, 100
Prayer, 67, 72–73, 109, 114
Premortal life, 7, 11, 29, 127, 143
Preparation, 14, 63–65
Pride, 119
Privacy, 10
Protection, divine, 92

Psalms, 86
Punishment, 24

Rachel, 147
Rebecca, 147
Relief Society, 35
Repentance, 93
Resentment, 135
Rob, story of, 33–35, 108–12, 149–50
Roman soldiers, 24

Sacrament, 34, 73
Sacrifice, 11, 66
Salvation, 10
Sarah, 140, 147
Satan: failed his first estate, 8; offered to remove risk, 17; plotting of, 22–23, 27; hopes we will despair, 49
Scott, story of, 69–70
Scripture study, 67, 72–73, 111–12
Second estate. *See* Mortal life
"Second yes," 57–59
Selfishness, 64
Self-pity, 60, 61
Sharon, story of, 107–8, 151
Smith, Joseph: in Liberty Jail, 1, 126–27; on happiness, 9; urged to endure, 37; faith of, 48, 50
Smith, Joseph Fielding, on guilt, 119
Solomon, 13
Souls, 77–79
Spirits, 122
Spirit world, 90

Spite, 22
Strength, 122–24
Suffer, meaning of, 48–49
Suffering: deserves thought, 2; meaning in, 10; is the price of friendship, 25; of Job, 42; enduring, 46–47; making sense of, 53, 151; and hope, 60; and fear, 63; as an offering, 66; combined, 80; and Jesus Christ, 138
Surgery, story of, 112–13
Sympathy, 54

Talmage, James E., on the mortal body, 143
Taming, 45–46
Tammy, story of, 70–73, 151
Temptation, 126
Terah, 10
Trials, 9–11, 24, 90
Tribulation, 64
Troubles, 144–45
Truth, 52

Veil, 138
Vic, story of, 106–7, 151

Weakness, 19–21, 87
Weariness, 46–47
Weight lifter analogy, 48–50
Wisdom, 13, 60
Work, 45–47
Worth, 77–79

Zeal, 104